The Rockhound's Guide
to MONTANA

by
Robert Feldman

FALCON™

Falcon Press® Publishing Co., Inc.
Helena, Montana

Front Cover: Photo by Darrin A. Schreder, Eldorado Bar Sapphire Mine.
Back Cover: Photo by Michael S. Sample. Materials provided by Tom Harmon
of Crane, Montana (Montana agate cabochons), Hal Hendrickson, Greenleaf's,
Billings, Montana (Yogo sapphires and gold nuggets), and Bob Feldman (all
other materials).

Library of Congress Cataloging-in-Publication Data

Feldman, Robert (Bob).
    The rockhound's guide to Montana / Robert Feldman.—
Billings, Mont. : Falcon Press Pub. Co., c1985.
        156 p. : ill., maps ; 23 cm.
        Includes bibliographies.
        ISBN 0-934318-46-8 (pbk.)

    1. Rocks—Montana—Collection and preservation. 2. Minerals—Montana
—Collection and preservation. 3. Fossils—Montana—Collection and preserva-
ion. I. Title.
    QE445.M9F45   1985   84-82466
    552.097896—dc19   CIP

Printed in the United States of America.

Falcon Press Publishing Co., Inc.
P.O. Box 1718, Helena, MT 59624

Photos by the author unless otherwise stated.

♻Text pages printed on Recycled Paper.

ACKNOWLEDGMENTS

Space and time will not permit me to adequately thank or even begin to thank everyone who helped in the making of this book. To those who furnished bits of information and a great deal of moral support, I offer my extreme gratitude. I would, however, like to specifically thank several persons, organizations, and businesses—Mr. David Lentfer, Mr. Ruel Janson, Mr. George Mitchell, Mr. John Schulte, Koop's Gems Rock Shop in Butte, Butler's Custom Faceting and Lapidary Supplies in Great Falls, and the various rock clubs in the state. Mr. LeRoy Anderson, Mr. Marshall Lambert, Mr. Mac McCurdy, and Mr. Henry Pope were all very gracious in providing special tours of the museums with which they are associated.

I of course want to thank my family for support and patience during the development of this book. I would also like to thank the late Tom McCann for his companionship and assistance on many field trips. It was an honor to spend time with this very fine gentleman.

I especially would like to extend my appreciation to my father, the late Howard Feldman. His encouragement and able assistance in the field during the years I pursued my geological studies will always be remembered. He was more than just a companion. He was a true friend and I miss him very much. I therefore dedicate this book to him and I hope that it will in some way offer others a start in a most interesting hobby, one that he and I together enjoyed and shared for many years.

DEDICATION

"To my dad. He was my best friend and a true rockhound."

CONTENTS

Museums with Displays of Rocks, Minerals,

A family looks for sapphires at the El Dorado Sapphire Mine. Darrin A. Schreder photo.

INTRODUCTION

"In all things of Nature there is something of the marvelous." Aristotle *(384-322 B.C.)*

A profusion of adjectives usually dominates brochures about Montana. It is true that Montana offers much aesthetically, but there is more than just what is seen on the surface of the land. There are both beauty and stories from the past hidden from view in Montana's rocks.

Montana has been an extremely important source of mineral wealth. The state's early history is focused around mining camps, most of which now fall to ruin in quiet mountain valleys. The recent increase in the price of gold has provided the impetus for new exploration of this rare, yellow metal. The ores of many different metals have been and will continue to be mined as our demands for natural resources increase.

There are minerals here in abundance. For years, lapidary artists have fashioned exquisite jewelry from some of the most unusual semi-precious and precious gemstones to be found anywhere in the world. The famous Montana agate, with its bands of red and brown and its fern-like dendrites, adorns belt buckles, bola ties, and pendants. The pride of owning a genuine Montana Yogo sapphire is perhaps surpassed only by the ownership of a self-found, self-faceted sapphire from one of the state's several public fee digging areas.

Some of the geologic past's most fascinating and grotesque creatures were discovered in the hardened sediments of ancient flood plains or seas which once existed here. Significant discoveries about Montana's geologic past continue to be made through the perseverence and insight of dedicated amateurs and trained professionals.

Rocks which were once molten, and those changed by forces deep within the earth's crust, provide the minerals upon which man is dependent. These same rocks often reveal beautiful crystalline aggregates of many more "nonessential" minerals. Such specimens commonly decorate the shelves of display cabinets in many large museums and private collections.

Mineral Collecting

Mineral production has represented one of Montana's major contributions to society, and since the late 1800's the state has witnessed the birth and death of many mining enterprises. Some have continued to be productive up to the present, but fluctuating markets and reserve uncertainties have closed most mines.

The abandoned mines of western Montana can provide rockhounds with an ideal source of mineral specimens. Sulfides such as pyrite, galena, and sphalerite along with quartz are the most common minerals to be found in the dumps and tailings of the mines worked for metals. At times, rare and uncommon minerals are also found, but only careful searching will reveal them. Some of the mines in the state were operated specifically for non-metallic minerals such as gem and abrasive corundum, optical calcite, talc, graphite, asbestos, and barite, just to name a few, and specimens of these minerals can still be found at these old mines. The rockhound who specializes in collecting the "flowers" of the mineral world will certainly enjoy these areas of Montana.

Although emphasis has been placed on collecting minerals from mines in western Montana, some exceptional crystalline varieties of nonmetallic minerals occur in the sedimentary rocks of eastern and central Montana. Cavities and vugs in limestone can produce superb crystals of calcite, and the fossil-bearing concretions common in exposures of marine shales contain delicate crystals of calcite, barite, and, rarely, some zeolite minerals.

Fossil Collecting

The landscape of Montana has changed throughout geologic time. Land areas rose and fell, and vast seas invaded and then retreated. This resulted in the formation of layers of rock, one atop another, each possessing characteristics of the conditions under which it was deposited. In them the remains of plants and animals were preserved, and a procession of different life forms is evident as the layers of rock are studied in sequence.

Brachiopods, corals, and crinoid remains are common fossils in marine limestones and shales of Cambrian, Devonian, and Mississippian ages, exposed on the margins of mountain ranges. Marine sediments of Jurassic age in central and southern Montana yield abundant fossils. Most common are the cigar-shaped belemnites, assorted oyster shells, and the star-shaped columnals of crinoids. The terrestrial sediments of Jurassic and Cretaceous formations such as the Morrison, Cloverly, Judith River, and Hell Creek contain the remains of many species of dinosaurs. Some of the world's most famous discoveries have been made in outcrops of these rocks in Montana. The marine shales of Cretaceous age in the eastern and central part of the state continue to be a source of spectacular ammonites. Coal mining in the Cenozoic sediments

Montana's western mountains have been a source of minerals.

3

Montana Agate can be fashioned into exquisite jewelry.

of eastern Montana implies the abundance of past vegetation. Beautifully preserved impressions of leaves and the logs and stumps of petrified trees occur in the rocks associated with the coal beds. There are also reported occurrences of fossil reptiles and mammals from these same rocks.

Some of eastern Montana has been referred to as "dinosaur graveyards." The finding of dinosaur remains can be exciting, to say the least, but it can also be frustrating. Seldom does the amateur have the equipment or educational background to properly collect such a fossil and interpret the sediments in which it is contained. It is of course tempting, but perhaps the collecting of these fossils should be left to the professional paleontologist so that an important find is not inadvertently destroyed. It is hoped that amateur fossil collectors will report significant finds to the proper authorities.

Gemstone Collecting

Gemstones are minerals or rocks which possess beauty, durability, and rarity. They are basically classified as two types, precious and semi-precious. Precious gemstones are much more rare and durable than semi-precious ones. Montana has classic examples of each. The state's official gemstones, the

Montana agate and the Montana sapphire, described in more detail later in this book, are some of the more prized gemstones to be found anywhere in the world. The Dryhead agate of southern Montana, because of its unusual pattern and uncommon nature, is of extreme value to collectors everywhere. Gem quality almandine garnets frequent the gravels of streams in southwestern Montana, and enjoyable hours can be spent in a historic atmosphere searching for them. An abundance of siliceous rocks with lapidary qualities prevail in outcrops and stream gravels throughout the state. Even some petrified wood, normally thought of as a fossil, is often fashioned into jewelry because of its "gemmy" quality. Several occurrences of amethyst and rock crystal have been, and continue to be, exploited as sources of gem material.

Gold Prospecting

GOLD! The mere mention of this word instills within people a desire to explore and seek the riches which lie hidden in the crust of the earth. It was this very desire which led to the settlement of Montana.

In 1852, placer gold was discovered on Gold Creek near the present town of Garrison. This discovery was quickly followed by the location of rich placer deposits near Bannack, which was to become the state's first territorial capital. Nearby, Virginia City and Alder Gulch were soon to prove their worth, and the mining of lode deposits began to accompany the placer operations. Millions of dollars worth of gold were recovered by such methods.

The operations were eventually halted by the combination of a fixed price of gold and rising operating costs, but there is still gold to be found in many of the old placer deposits and mines. Panning gold for hobby purposes on public land without staking a mining claim is generally permitted. Larger scale operations, such as dredging or sluicing, require special permits. Many streams in western Montana provide the ideal setting for panning gold; a few streams which are known producers of small quantities of placer gold are mentioned in various locality descriptions in this book.

Several books written by Montana authors discuss methods of locating and recovering gold. One written by Gregory Stone and another written by Verne Ballantyne are highly recommended to the reader who wishes to hobby pan for gold in Montana. To help find areas where hobby panning may yield gold, the reader should see Montana Bureau of Mines and Geology Memoir 5, *Placer Mining Possibilities in Montana*, by O. A. Dingman, and Memoir 26, *The Gold Placers of Montana*, by Charles J. Lyden. *Gold Secrets of Mystical Montana: A Manual for the Recreational Prospector*, by James E. Hanson, is a compilation of information from Montana Bureau of Mines and Geology publications and other sources. Bureau of Land Management and National Forest Service maps of western Montana will help keep you oriented as to the ownership status of the land.

Both Mr. Stone's and Mr. Ballantyne's books will be useful to those who wish to pursue the search for gold beyond the hobby panning stage. Also recommended are Montana Bureau of Mines and Geology Bulletin 22, *Montana Mining Law*, by K.S. Stout, and Bulletin 99, *Handbook for Small Mining Enterprises*, by F.N. Earll.

"Spelunking"

Montana has many caves. A few of the more well known are briefly described in this book. The enthusiastic spelunker is referred to Montana

Bureau of Mines and Geology Bulletin 105, *Caves of Montana*, by N. P. Campbell. This publication provides the information one would need to explore caves in the state, which often exhibit beautiful and unusual crystalline deposits of calcite, gypsum, and ice. Every rockhound is encouraged to visit the caverns offering guided tours, if only to briefly witness this aspect of the rock hobby.

A reminder, however: These unusual and often spectacular features took hundreds of years to form. It is hoped that rockhounds will not vandalize them for their own selfish purposes, but help to protect them for the enjoyment of others.

Collecting Techniques

Sometimes a collector finds well preserved specimens lying loose on the surface. For the most part, though, specimens usually need to be removed from the host rock and prepared in some fashion before being displayed in a collection. This is especially true for fine crystals and many fossils.

Three books on collecting techniques have been particularly useful to this writer. *The Handbook of Crystal and Mineral Collecting,* by William Sanborn, and *Prospecting for Gemstones and Minerals,* by John Sinkankas, have been handy guides to follow when collecting, preparing, and displaying minerals. The methods they present are appropriate regardless of where one searches for and finds minerals. *Fossils For Amateurs,* by Russell MacFall and Jay Wollin, is an excellent resource for the rockhound collecting fossils. It provides a considerable amount of information concerning the kinds of rocks in which fossils are found and the methods by which they should be collected, prepared, and displayed.

Using This Book

Montana—a rockhound's paradise? Perhaps! Montana has many potential sources of interesting minerals, fossils, and gemstones. This book has been written as a guide and attempts to emphasize all aspects of the rock hobby as they pertain to Montana.

An abbreviated discussion of some of Montana's geologic history is presented in the next section. A simplified geologic time scale is provided to help orient the reader to the various time periods and their relationship to one another. Additional but very simplified geologic information is also presented in other sections of the book as it becomes necessary.

Agates and sapphires are perhaps the most sought after rock hobby materials the state has to offer, and as a result, they were officially designated the state gemstones. The section entitled Montana's Official State Gemstones briefly discusses the suggested origins and histories of these most interesting and valuable gem materials.

Even though most seasoned rockhounds are more than likely aware of their obligations to the rock hobby, it is necessary to discuss some of the innumerable rules and regulations by which rockhounds must abide. General information regarding access to various lands within the state is presented in Rules and Regulations for Rockhounds. It also provides some specific details concerning the collecting of certain rock hobby materials such as petrified wood and other fossils on public land. More rockhounds need to become particularly concerned about their hobby and commit themselves to preserving their privilege to collect on private as well as on public land.

Since most rockhounds want to collect their own material, Localities of Interest in Montana will more than likely be of particular interest. A number of popular fee and nonfee collecting localities are presented. A continued conservative attitude on the part of rockhounds will allow these areas to continue to produce high quality rock hobby materials. Many of the localities not only have good collecting potential, but they are also areas of geological interest. A number of the major mining districts in the state are included as localities because the dumps and tailings of the mines have, in the past, produced fine crystals of rare and unusual minerals. The potential of these areas can of course be damaged by ignoring the rules and regulations discussed in Rules and Regulations for Rockhounds.

The various locality descriptions are generally accompanied by relatively detailed maps, but this should not mislead one to assume that this automatically grants access. It definitely does not! The vast majority of the mineral deposits, fossil beds, and gemstone localities described in this book occur on private or claimed property, and access is by permission of the landowner or claimholder only. Many good collecting sites have been permanently closed because of failure by some individuals to secure permission to enter private property or mining claims, or to abide by the rules and regulations which were applicable in those situations. The importance of meeting our obligations as rockhunters cannot be overemphasized.

Several methods can be used to obtain land owner information. One can inquire at nearby towns, and the county treasurer's office can often provide private landowner's names, if the legal description of the property (quarter section, township, and range) can be provided. Detailed Bureau of Land Management, USDA Forest Service, and U.S. Geological Survey maps can be helpful in determining legal descriptions of land. The Bureau of Land Management also keeps a current listing of persons owning mining claims in the state. Again, all that is needed to determine ownership is the legal description of the land on which the mining claim is located. For convenience, each locality description in this book has a listing of useful maps if any are available. Also, for those who might wish to obtain more information concerning a specific locality, a list of available references (many of them technical) which deal with the locality or adjacent areas is provided.

Brief descriptions of some museums and public displays in Montana with items of special interest to rockhounds appear in the last section. The season and operating hours are shown for convenience, and a mailing address is also furnished in case the reader would like to write for additional information. Most of the museums which have been considered here have displays of minerals, fossils, gemstone material, and artifacts which have been collected locally. These displays can show rockhounds typical examples of specimens of that area as well as some of the items protected by law, which are therefore uncollectable. The curators and workers at these museums are excellent resource people and can often provide information concerning the status of nearby collecting areas.

A sequence of appendices at the back of the book provides some incidental information. This includes a listing of general references (Appendix A), rock shops (Appendix B), active rock clubs (Appendix C), and specific agencies in Montana which can provide information relevant to the rock hobby (Appendix D).

It is obvious though, that a book of this size is incapable of presenting or discussing the entire rock hobby potential of Montana. It instead has been designed to be your introduction to the state's minerals, fossils, and gemstones. Let your own ingenuity and expertise build on what this book has to offer, and enjoy the good fortune that has satisfied others while they pursued the "treasures" to be found in Montana.

MONTANA'S GEOLOGICAL STORY

"Time which antiquates, and hath an art to make dust of all things" Sir Thomas Browne (1605-1682)

The physiography of Montana is extremely varied. The western mountains stand in stark contrast to the eastern plains. Apparently, different geologic processes have acted throughout time on the rocks of these regions.

Landscapes changed. As seas transgressed and regressed across the face of the land, sediments piled up in layers of great thickness, recording, like pages in a book, the histories of earlier times. The more or less horizontal layers of sandstone and shale in eastern Montana indicate very little disturbance since their initial deposition millions of years ago, but the rugged mountains to the west furnish evidence of tremendous diastrophic forces. Time and the elements have changed this land, and what is now a cliff face on a mountain top may have been an ocean floor during an earlier geologic period.

Investigations of some of the complex and highly altered Precambrian metamorphic rocks in many of Montana's mountain ranges indicate that they were once soft mud and sand deposited in or adjacent to seas. Exactly what these areas were like during those periods is not known. The fascinating story contained in these rocks is difficult to interpret. Because the rocks are so altered and deformed, it is virtually impossible for geologists to determine the source of the sediments which became the gneisses and schists we see today. Montana's physical geography during that period of time will, for the most part, remain a mystery.

Though not yet totally understood, younger Precambrian rocks reveal some of their history a little more freely. A group called the Belt Series, composed of slightly altered sandstones and shales, tells of an ancient sea which occupied most of western and central Montana. These rocks are unique in that they are composed entirely of very shallow water sediments, showing mud cracks, ripple marks, cross bedding, and other very shallow water sedimentary features. The vast thickness of these rocks in western Montana leads geologists to believe they were deposited on the floor of an ocean basin that was slowly subsiding. Fossils in the Belt Series rocks are limited to very primitive organisms. Unusual occurrences of algae in the Glacier Park area are probably the most spectacular fossils to be found in Precambrian rocks of Montana.

Throughout the Paleozoic Era the seas advanced and withdrew numerous times. Unlike Precambrian rocks, Paleozoic rocks contain a relative abundance of fossils, and geologists have been able to use them to correlate the general movement of the ancient seas in which they were deposited. Although it has not been determined how the land masses actually appeared, there is general agreement concerning their locations during this era. Apparently, there was minimal diastrophic activity in Montana then, but even that little was responsible for the gradual change visible today in a section of Paleozoic rocks. In some areas the changes were significant enough to cause certain rock units to be missing from the sequence, possibly as a result of erosion or even non-deposition. Outcrops of Paleozoic formations are largely confined to the margins of the mountain areas where fairly recent mountain building has arched the layers and erosion has exposed them. Fossils are common in these outcrops and are essentially represented by marine animals such as brachiopods, bryozoans, crinoids, and trilobites. Paleozoic rocks buried beneath much of central and eastern Montana have also provided a great deal of the oil extracted from the state.

The seas continued to move back and forth during the Mesozoic Era. Conditions were favorable for the existence of dinosaurs and several rock units have yielded the remains of *Tyrannosaurus rex, Triceratops,* and many species of *Hadrosaurs* (duck-bills). Of the Late Mesozoic rocks exposed at the surface today, marine sediments are probably the most extensive.

A study of these sediments and the fossils they contain indicates that they accumulated as fine-grained sediments over a lengthy time period when a broad, north-south trending inland sea occupied a good portion of central North America. The sea grew and shrank many times producing alternating layers of sandstone and shale in central Montana. The major source of the sediments being deposited here was a mountainous highland to the west, probably in the general vicinity of the present day Rocky Mountains.

The rocks produced by this deposition have provided some spectacular fossils. Even though the remains of swimming vertebrate animals such as *Mosasaurs* and *Pleisiosaurs* are sometimes found, the most common animals found in Mesozoic rocks are mollusks. Of these, perhaps the most fascinating are the ammonites, relatives of the present day chambered nautilus. In fact, ammonites are probably one of the more prized fossils to be placed in a collection.

The seas had gradually retreated from the continent by Early Cenozoic time. The advance of this era brought about the extinction of many life-forms such as the dinosaurs and ammonites, their demise still much of a mystery. Many of these life forms were highly specialized organisms, and, as highly specialized organisms ourselves, perhaps we can benefit from studies of them.

In the Early Tertiary Period eastern and central Montana accumulated large quantities of vegetation, the source of extensive present-day deposits of bituminous and sub-bituminous coal and lignite. The forests were primarily a hardwood type, and the landscape was relatively low and flat, perhaps similar to the Mississippi River Delta region today. Crocodiles, turtles, and other vertebrates swam in the numerous stream channels which criss-crossed the landscape, and their remains have been found in sandstone beds adjacent to coal beds near Miles City and Terry. Later as the land steadily rose with the development of the Rocky Mountains, the carving action of rivers and glaciers produced the Montana we know today.

The geologic history of Montana is difficult to interpret, and these few paragraphs obviously cannot adequately describe it. Unfortunately, there is no single publication available at present which does so. *Roadside Geology of*

Specimens of Baculites, *the most common ammonite in Cretaceous rocks of central and eastern Montana, often reveal beautiful suture patterns.*

Montana, by David Alt and Donald Hyndman, is an excellent reference for interpreting geologic features observable from Montana's major roadways. Numerous collecting sites are also briefly mentioned, some of which are presented in slightly more detail than this book. Montana Bureau of Mines and Geology Bulletin 26, *Montana in the Geologic Past,* by Eugene Perry, is a good general reference. It is easy to read and provides considerable information to those with little geologic training, but production data for minerals and fossil fuels is now outdated. A third good source of general information can be found in many of the earlier issues of *Montana Magazine.* The magazine used to regularly feature articles for the lay person on some specific aspect of Montana geology, usually with an emphasis on the geologic origins of the more spectacular and well known landforms. For more detailed geologic information consult the more technical publications of the Montana Bureau of Mines and Geology and the United States Geological Survey.

Sound background in geology is helpful in order to understand and appreciate the intricate processes which have changed and shaped Montana. With this background, geologists are able to read and interpret the layered sedimentary rocks of the plains and the complex igneous and metamorphic rocks of the mountains in an attempt to piece together a most intriguing story, one which is unsurpassed by any best selling novel.

It is a continuing study, though, for not all of the pages of rock history have been interpreted, nor have all the questions been answered. This is why the study of geology is so fascinating to the rockhound. There is so much yet to be explored and discovered. For years, sincere and dedicated rockhounds have assisted the professional earth scientists by making discoveries and contributing to the ever growing list of new minerals and fossils. It is of the utmost impor-

Simplified Geologic Time Table

Era	Period	Epoch	Major Event
Cenozoic	Quaternary	Recent (10,000) Pleistocene (2,000,000)	Ice Ages
	Tertiary	Pliocene (11,000,000) Miocene (25,000,000) Oligocene (40,000,000) Eocene (60,000,000) Paleocene (70,000,000)	Age of Mammals
Mesozoic	Cretaceous (135,000,000) Jurassic (180,000,000) Triassic (225,000,000)		Age of Dinosaurs
Paleozoic	Permian (270,000,000) Pennsylvanian (305,000,000) Mississippian (350,000,000) Devonian (400,000,000) Silurian (440,000,000) Ordovician (500,000,000) Cambrian (600,000,000)		Age of Invertebrates
Precambrian	Proterozoic (2,500,000,000) Archeozoic (4,500,000,000)		Earliest Life (3,200,000,000)

(Numbers refer to years before present)

Outcrops of Cretaceous shales and sandstones in central and southern Montana contain well preserved fossils.

tance then, that rockhounds realize their potential and continue to work positively with the professional geologists.

MONTANA'S OFFICIAL STATE GEMSTONES

"In the vaunted works of Art, the master stroke is Nature's part" Ralph Waldo Emerson (1803-1882)

The agate and the sapphire are important gemstones. Agates have been collected for many years from the gravels of eastern Montana, and since the late 1800's sapphires have been known to exist in the gold placer deposits of western Montana. Pressured by the various rock clubs in the state, the Montana Legislature passed legislation in 1969 making the agate and the sapphire the state's official gemstones. As a result they play a major role in attracting tourists.

Montana Agate

Montana agate occurs in a variety of patterns, from those with red and dark brown bands to the prized dendritic forms. It is the black "tree-like" design in the dendritic variety which has made Montana agate one of the most sought after agates in the nation. When viewing high quality dendritic Montana agate, the imagination can see beautiful lakes surrounded by dense forests, or the silhouette of some animal.

Agate is a variety of quartz, the second most abundant mineral in the earth's crust. But agate is not plentiful like ordinary quartz, and the fact that Montana agate is becoming increasingly difficult to find makes it even more valuable. The finding of Montana agate, like any good lapidary material, requires the knowledge of where to search and a good deal of perseverance. Do not expect to spend just a few hours in eastern Montana and find quantities of quality agate.

Many theories have been advanced regarding the origin of Montana agate. One "old timer" believed that the agate was initially formed like soft jelly on the ground. As it hardened into rock, a picture of the surrounding landscape formed within it. This, he said, explained the "trees" and shapes of birds and animals found in the agate when it is cut. The red and brown bands in much of the agate were explained as nothing more than the frozen reflection of a colorful sunset. The "pictures" are, in reality, shapes and patterns produced by dendrites of manganese dioxide and iron oxide which have been deposited in minute fractures.

The original source of Montana agate has also been a mystery, and as mentioned earlier, many theories have been proposed concerning its origin. It has been suggested that several factors imply an upper Yellowstone-Absaroka volcanic field origin. The rocks in this region contain chalcedony within cavities and vugs of volcanic rock, and noticeably, the eastern Montana agates occur in the gravel deposited by ancestral streams which had their headwaters in this region. The chalcedony of these volcanic rocks is for the most part, however, not completely like the "classic" Montana agate found in the gravels of eastern Montana—one of several contradicting factors.

The discovery of dendritic or "moss" agates occurring in a Tertiary volcanic ash bed of central Wyoming has prompted another theory. Perhaps the dendritic Montana agate may have formed in the same way. Since the dendritic Montana agate seems to occur most commonly in the Custer to Miles City area, it may have originated in Tertiary volcanic ash beds of the Tongue River,Powder River, and Big Horn River basins of southern Montana and northern Wyoming. These basins are drained by streams which flow into eastern Montana, and although no volcanic ash deposits containing moss agates occur there at present, it is possible that they may have once existed and have subsequently been obliterated by gradational processes.

Another theory suggests that the varieties of Montana agate were derived from glacial gravels carried southward by stream action following the Pleistocene glaciation. This would imply that the original source of the agate lies to the north in Canada, but so far no source has been found. With the

Montana agate exhibits a variety of patterns and designs

exception of the agate associated with some isolated gravel deposits in northeastern Montana and southern Canada, collectively referred to as the Flaxville Gravel, most of the agate lies generally to the south of the Yellowstone River. This in itself casts at least some doubt as to a glacial origin for the Montana agate.

Perhaps the agates originate from several sources. This would make a combination of the above explanations valid. The variation in the types of Montana agate to be found as one travels from southwest to northeast along the Yellowstone River does suggest more than one source. A knowledge of the original source of Montana agate and its distribution patterns may help geologists more accurately interpret the Late Cenozoic history of the Northern Plains Region.

Montana Sapphires

Sapphires are the blue-colored gem variety of corundum, an oxide of aluminum. Faceted, they are one of the most beautiful precious gemstones in existence, having adorned the crowns and scepters of royalty the world over.

Montana is one of three regions in the United States which has commercially produced corundum for use as either abrasives or as gemstones. In fact, the most spectacular gem locality in this country can be found in Montana. This of course, is the Yogo Sapphire locality, and although it is inaccessible to the collector, it is described later in this book because of its historical importance.

Throughout the state, where sapphires are found, they occur primarily in placer deposits. In some cases, these placer deposits have been traced to dikes and sills, implying an igneous origin.

A few of the commercial operations in the state also allow public digging for a fee. As a result of increased mining costs and inflation in general, fees for digging can change from year to year. It should be noted, however, that because of what may be found these fees are normally reasonable.

Experiencing the thrill of actually discovering their own sapphires is a rare opportunity offered to rockhounds. Many of the sapphires found are of facetable quality. The hobby of faceting gemstones is becoming increasingly popular and the sapphire mines of western Montana can provide a source of beautiful material with which to work.

Because of the quality of gem sapphires being discovered by rockhounds, many mine operators have considered closing their mines to public digging. This of course would be unfortunate for the rockhound, but it may also produce a potential problem for the mine operators. If gem sapphires were to flood the market, the price would no doubt plummet and mines may close as they did in the early 1900s. It is hoped that the mine operators will allow sapphire collecting to continue.

RULES AND REGULATIONS FOR ROCKHOUNDS — A REMINDER

"The Law is the last result of human wisdom acting upon human experience for the benefit of the Public" Samuel Johnson (1709-1784)

The American Federation of Mineralogical Societies has developed a code of ethics which rockhounds may follow in their attempts to secure rock hobby materials from various types of land. This code has been reprinted here with the permission of the federation. The importance of rock hobby ethics cannot be over emphasized.

AFMS Code of Ethics

I WILL respect both private and public property and will do no collecting on privately owned land without permission from the owner.

I WILL keep informed on all laws, regulations, and rules governing collecting on public lands and will observe them.

I WILL, to the best of my ability, ascertain the boundary lines of property on which I plan to collect.

I WILL use no firearms or blasting materials in collecting areas.

I WILL cause no willful damage to property of any kind, such as: fences, signs, buildings, etc.

I WILL leave all gates as found.

I WILL build fires only in designated or safe places and will be certain they are completely extinguished before leaving the area.

I WILL discard no burning materials—matches, cigarettes, etc.

I WILL fill all excavation holes which may be dangerous to livestock.

I WILL not contaminate wells, creeks or other water supplies.

I WILL cause no damage to collecting material and will take home only what I can reasonably use.

I WILL support the rockhound project H.E.L.P. (Help Eliminate Litter, Please) and will leave all collecting areas devoid of litter, regardless of how found.

I WILL cooperate with field trip leaders and those in designated authority in all collecting areas.

I WILL report to my club or federation officers, Bureau of Land Management, or other proper authority, any deposit of petrified wood or other material on public lands which should be protected for the enjoyment of future generations and for public educational and scientific purposes.

I WILL appreciate and protect our heritage of natural resources.

I WILL observe the "Golden Rule," use good outdoor manners and will at all times conduct myself in a manner which will add to the stature and public image of rockhounds everywhere.

Government regulations have been established in an attempt to preserve certain objects. The Federal Antiquities Act of 1906 specified that certain items of antiquity (mainly artifacts) found on public or federal lands could only be collected by qualified persons equipped with permits. The 1906 Act has been interpreted to include vertebrate and other fossils of scientific value. This interpretation is somewhat vague and therefore recently has been subjected to close inspection by scientific and commercial groups, resulting in the "Paleontological Conservation Act of 1983," which at the time of this writing was being introduced as S. 1659. Details of this proposed legislation can be found in Volume 129, No. 93 of the Congressional Record. The bill's general purpose is to simplify the rules and regulations presently used to protect vertebrate fossils and permit more professional collecting of such fossils. It even includes a provision for the collecting of some vertebrate fossils by amateurs. Invertebrate fossils, gemstones, and minerals are briefly mentioned in the bill, but apparently they would not be subject to permit collecting. If the bill is accepted and becomes federal law, it is hoped that amateur fossil collectors will still use common sense and report fossil finds of an unusual nature.

Several years ago, the Bureau of Land Management attempted to simplify its limited Rules of Conduct for Removing Geologic and Hobby Materials from Public Lands. The attempt was not well received by the rockhound community and a barrage of letters caused the BLM to at least temporarily table those revisions. For details concerning those proposed revisions, refer to the August 17, 1982 *Federal Register;* Vol. 47, No. 159, p. 35914-35917.

At present the collecting of certain fossils on public or federal lands can be done only with permits which are usually restricted and issued only to recognized scientific institutions such as museums or universities. In most cases, the importance of these types of regulations is obvious. Fossils and artifacts are some of the only clues we have to the history of our earth, and for that particular reason, it is necessary to see that they are properly collected and preserved. Serious rockhounds certainly do not wish to see important discoveries destroyed or abused. By reporting significant finds to the proper authorities, they can offer their contribution to the preservation of such finds.

The collecting of common fossils, minerals, and gemstones for hobby purposes is presently permitted on public lands as long as certain procedures are used. It must be pointed out, however, that popular rockhound areas located on public lands are subject to possible commercialism if the material being looked for is considered to be of marketable quality and quantity. It may behoove rockhounds therefore, to work through their local rock clubs and various government agencies to design a program where such areas can be protected and set aside for only hobby collecting, with limitations on commercial collecting.

Gaining access to some lands is sometimes difficult for rockhounds because of certain rules and laws. Many of these laws were developed to protect landowners, and fortunately, most rockhounds respect them. As mentioned earlier in the book, failure on the part of ignorant and irresponsible individuals has, over the years, resulted in the permanent closure of many fine collecting localities across our nation.

Rules which apply to hobby collecting of minerals, gemstones, and fossils on Bureau of Land Management land can differ from those dealing with state or National Forest Service land. Obviously, quite different rules apply regarding private land and mining claims. It is necessary then, to generally discuss some of the more important rules which at this time are relevant to hobby collecting of earth materials on the different types of land.

Bureau of Land Management Land

The BLM generally allows, with certain exceptions, the collecting of rocks, minerals, fossils, and gemstones on BLM lands for hobby purposes without a permit. The exceptions of course include the collecting of fossils or minerals of particular scientific importance, or the collecting of rock hobby materials in protected areas. Currently, the regulations allow no collecting of vertebrate fossils for hobby purposes but do allow the collecting of common invertebrate fossils. There has generally been no limit to the amount of rock hobby materials which may be collected, with the exception of fossil wood. The collecting of fossil wood on BLM land is still limited to twenty-five pounds per day per individual, not to exceed 250 pounds per year.

The BLM published a series of maps which can be particularly useful to the rockhound. Designed primarily for recreation, each map covers about 3,000 square miles (eighty townships) and shows, by section, the ownership status of the land (BLM, state, national forest, etc.), major campsites, recreational areas, and major roads and trails. Specific reference is made to appropriate BLM maps in each of the locality descriptions provided later in the book. They provide a useful reference if land ownership is to be determined for a particular area.

State Land

State land is administered somewhat differently than BLM land. Most state land in Montana has been leased by ranchers and various private enterprises. Where BLM-leased land is accessible without prior approval of the lessee, state property is not. State land which has been leased is treated much like private land, and one can be prosecuted for trespassing if permission has not been obtained from the lessee.

The rules and regulations regarding the removal of fossils, minerals, and gemstones from state land are also quite different than those concerning BLM land. The state restricts the collecting of any rock hobby materials, and in particular precious metals and gemstones. The legal collecting of rock hobby materials is a different process and the interested reader is advised to contact a state land administrative office for further information concerning access to state lands for rock hobby purposes.

Tribal Land

Considerable areas of Montana have been set aside for many different tribes of Native Americans. It is imperative that proper procedures be followed when attempting to gain access to these lands.

Initially, one should contact the Office of the Superintendent of the Bureau of Indian Affairs administering the reservation on which the site in question is located. Permission to collect rock hobby materials will either be granted or denied, or the appropriate information will be provided. If your request is approved, permission must still be obtained from the specific owner or lessee of the land where the collecting would take place.

USDA Forest Service Land

If pursued as a general recreational activity, the collecting of minerals, rocks, gemstones, and common fossils is permitted on USDA Forest Service land without a permit. This also includes hobby panning for gold. Permits are required, however, for the collecting of specimens for commercial use, large quantities of a particular rock type for personal use (fireplaces, patios, etc.), and petrified wood (see locality description for the Gallatin Petrified Forest later in this book for details). A mining claim must be filed and Montana mining law obeyed if the search for precious metals (gold, silver, etc.) or gemstones goes beyond the recreational activity state.

It must also be pointed out that the USDA Forest Service strictly enforces the Federal Antiquities Act of 1906 and various federal regulations codes with regard to fossils of scientific importance and artifacts or materials which have been worked and manipulated by man.

The USDA Forest Service, too, publishes maps which can be useful to rockhounds, particularly with reference to the western part of the state.

Other Federal Land

National parks, monuments, and wildlife refuges are protected by acts of Congress. The collecting of specimens of any nature is allowed only by permit, and permits are issued only for qualified scientific research. Regulations are generally based on the various interpretations of the Federal Antiquities Act of 1906 and certain parts of the Code of Federal Regulations (specifically, CFR 43, part 3, and CFR 50, parts 27. 62 and 27.63).

Private Land

Since many excellent collecting areas for earth materials are found on private land, it is very important that permission to enter be obtained. Without it, the trespasser may be prosecuted. More importantly, the landowner could close his land to all collecting.

Mining Claims

Can you be shot for trespassing on a mining claim without permission? It was perhaps a common event in Montana's early mining history, for "claim jumpers" were not treated well by claim holders. There have been incidents of persons being shot at while searching what appeared to be abandoned mine dumps for mineral specimens. Mines which appear abandoned may not be, or they may be on private property.

If permission is obtained to enter the property on which a mine is located, the following should be kept in mind. Many of these mines have not been operated for several decades and hazards abound. Rotting timbers, poisonous gases, and denning wild animals are just a few reasons why mine shafts and tunnels should not be entered. Many vertical shafts which are only partially caved dot the landscape in some mining regions, so care must be taken not to stumble into one. Some of them descend for more than one hundred feet.

With the exception of the minerals sought at the time the mine was active, most minerals encountered in the mine can usually be found to some degree in the dumps and tailings. The passage of time and the agents of weathering have, for the most part, altered those on the surface of the dumps, but careful searching will often disclose fine specimens suitable for micromount or thumbnail collections.

LOCALITIES OF INTEREST IN MONTANA

"Oh lord, how manifold are thy works! In wisdom hast thou made them all: the earth is full of thy riches" The Holy Bible: Psalms 104:24

The following chapter describes localities where interesting rock hobby materials can be found. Several factors govern the productivity of a potential collecting site. One is accessibility—many of the areas described are on private or claimed land and access may be denied. Another is the degree to which the site has been collected in the past, since weathering and erosional processes are slow and new material is exposed only by time. Another is the amount of time budgeted by the collector. Hours or even days of unrelenting pursuit may be necessary before preferred specimens are found.

A number of general areas are discussed and specific localities within those areas are described in some detail. If the locality is within a mining district, some of the history of the mining activity in the district is provided along with some minimal geological information. The description of each locality also includes access (private land, BLM land, etc.), a listing of available published maps, and a list of references which describe the area in more detail. Many of the references are technical and appropriate to rockhounds versed in the many fields of geology. Each described locality is also accompanied by a map showing the nearest town or noticeable landmarks—a good Montana highway map will aid in locating the general area.

Sand and gravel bars along the Yellowstone River in eastern Montana are a source of Montana agate and other lapidary material.

Montana Agate Along The Yellowstone River

As described earlier, Montana agate is one of the state's official gemstones, and good quality pieces are highly prized. Specific localities at which Montana agate can be found are virtually impossible to present since it is generally widespread throughout eastern Montana. It occurs primarily in terrace gravel deposits high on the hills above the Yellowstone River and its tributaries, as well as in the sand and gravel bars within the streams themselves.

The terrace deposits above and adjacent to the rivers and streams are often not easily accessible because they mostly occur on private land. Be sure that permission has been obtained from the landowner before collecting there. Members of the Yellowstone Agate Club in Miles city, the Glendive Rock and Hobby Club in Glendive, and the proprietors of rock shops in towns along the Yellowstone River may be able to provide information concerning areas which are accessible.

Finding agate involves a careful study of the gravels as one walks over them. The blue-gray color and translucency of chalcedony usually identifies an agate. Agates found in the terrace deposits frequently possess a "whitewashed" appearance but this is not necessarily a criterion for spotting agates since many of the siliceous rocks such as jasper, quartz, and even petrified wood have the same coating. Most of the agate which is found will lack the beautiful patterns and designs of prized agates, but here is where perseverance pays off. Continuous searching is what finds quality agate.

Since the gravels within streams and rivers are constantly shifting and being reworked, these are probably the best areas to search. To do this, however, one must often "float" the rivers or streams, and unless you are skilled at floating rivers, this can be hazardous. Certain precautions and preparations are also necessary, and it would be wise to check locally before taking such a venture. It is suggested that you again contact any one of the rock clubs or rock shops in towns along the Yellowstone River east of Billings. *The Floater's Guide to Montana,* by Hank Fischer can also provide some very helpful

MONTANA AGATE COUNTRY

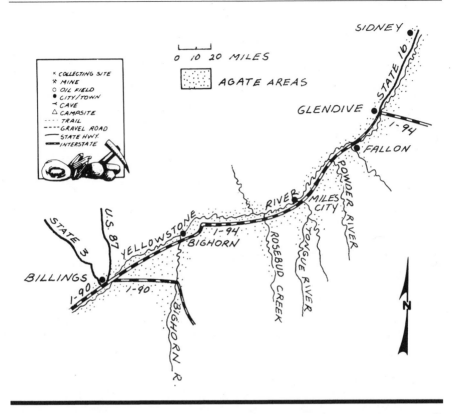

information with regard to floating rivers. Although the Yellowstone River is available for public use, access to it is sometimes difficult as there are few places where a boat or raft of any size can be launched.

Floating the river allows one to search the many sand and gravel bars along the shore as well as those exposed in midstream. Searching here for agate can be difficult, however, since moss and algae sometime coat the rocks as high water subsides in late spring. One should also keep in mind that others will be searching for agate in this fashion, and therefore the earlier in spring or early summer one can begin searching, the better.

Once access has been gained to either the river gravels or terrace gravels, success merely depends on your skill in recognizing agates. The agate-bearing gravels also contain boulders and cobbles of fine red jasper and petrified wood. Like the agate, not all of this material is suitable for lapidary purposes, but much of it is extremely colorful when cut and polished. If you are not successful in finding agate, remember that there are many rockshops throughout Montana which sell rough Montana agate and finished Montana agate jewelry.

Access Information: Private land, BLM land.

Useful Maps: BLM Public Lands in Montana maps: 20 *Savage,* 27 *Sumatra,* 28 *Rosebud,* 29 *Custer,* 30 *Fallon,* 36 *Pryor.*

Specific References:

Anderson, J.W. "Along the Yellowstone There's More Than Agates," *Lapidary Journal,* Vol 27, No. 4, July, 1973, pp. 616-619.

Fischer, Hank. *The Floater's Guide to Montana,* Helena, Montana, Falcon Press Publishing Co., Inc., 1980, pp. 124-13 1 .

Harmon, Tom. "Hunting The Yellowstone for Moss Agate." *Gems and Minerals,* No. 503, September, 1979, pp. 84-85.

Prchal, Marshall. "Montana's Dendritic Moss Agate—Is It All Gone?" *Lapidary Journal,* Vol. 22, No. 5, August, 1968, pp. 620-631.

Young, M. W. "A Yellowstone Float Trip," *Gems and Minerals,* No. 430, July, 1973, pp. 30-31.

Fossils Near Glendive

The Plains Indians called them "Maco-Sica." We call them badlands. Composed mainly of soft shales and sandstones, the sediments of the Tertiary Fort Union Formation and the Cretaceous Hell Creek Formation in eastern Montana are easily affected by the agents of weathering and erosion.

Sculptured by running water, Makoshika State Park near Glendive is a spectacular example of badlands topography. The various layers of sedimentary rock are well exposed and fossils have been collected and studied here for many years. The remains of fossil plants, dinosaurs, and small mammals, some exceedingly rare, have been removed from these beds.

Collecting of common fossils in the park is not allowed without a permit, and encounters with rare or unusual fossils should be reported. Some of the more interesting fossils worth searching for are leaf prints in the sandstone and shale layers of the Fort Union Formation, and the fossil "figs" and reversed casts of pine cones in the Hell Creek Formation. The sandstone casts called "figs" have the same general shape as present day figs, but their actual identity continues to be debated by paleobotanists. Careful observation of the individual rock layers and detailed scrutiny of broken rock fragments will aid in the search for fossils here.

The park is situated southeast of Glendive and can be reached with only a few minutes drive. From the downtown section of Glendive drive south on Merrill Avenue to Barry Street, turn left, and proceed under the railroad overpass. Drive four blocks to Taylor Avenue, turn right and proceed another six blocks to Snyder Street. Turn left and, within a mile or so, you will reach Makoshika State Park. Several maintained and unmaintained roads lead to the park's interior.

If you are pulling a trailer of any sort, it would be advisable to leave it at a local campground if you plan to spend more than a day. Negotiating the twists and turns made by the roads is virtually impossible with a trailer in tow. There is a parking area for trailers at the base of the "switchbacks" as you first enter, but camping facilities here are very primitive.

A very informative pamphlet written by Dr. R. W. Hiatt on the natural history of Makoshika State Park may still be available through the Glendive Chamber for one who is not familiar with the area.

GLENDIVE AREA

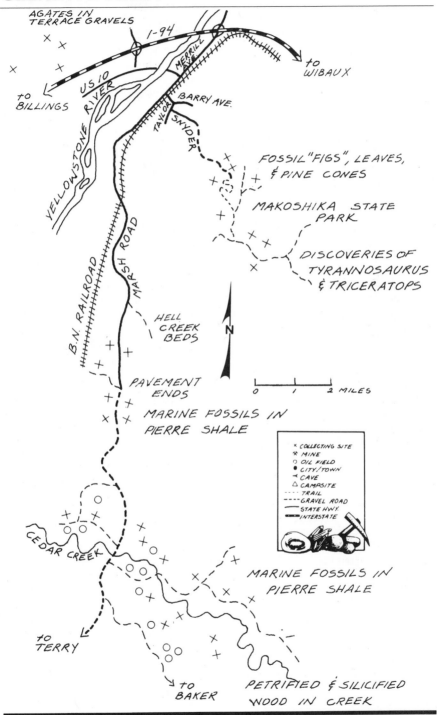

AGATES IN TERRACE GRAVELS

I-94

US 10

to BILLINGS

to WIBAUX

MERRILL AVE.

BARRY AVE.

TAYLOR

SNYDER

YELLOWSTONE RIVER

FOSSIL "FIGS", LEAVES, & PINE CONES

MAKOSHIKA STATE PARK

DISCOVERIES OF TYRANNOSAURUS & TRICERATOPS

B.N. RAILROAD

MARSH ROAD

HELL CREEK BEDS

N

PAVEMENT ENDS

MARINE FOSSILS IN PIERRE SHALE

0   1   2 MILES

× COLLECTING SITE
✶ MINE
○ OIL FIELD
● CITY/TOWN
⌐ CAVE
△ CAMPSITE
⋯ TRAIL
--- GRAVEL ROAD
─── STATE HWY.
━━━ INTERSTATE

CEDAR CREEK

MARINE FOSSILS IN PIERRE SHALE

to TERRY

to BAKER

PETRIFIED & SILICIFIED WOOD IN CREEK

Outcrops of the Late Cretaceous Pierre Shale occur in roadcuts, bluffs, and stream banks along Cedar Creek south of Glendive. Only the uppermost portion of the entire sequence of strata in the Pierre Shale is exposed and so the fauna which can be collected is limited in variety. Among the fossils to be found here are numerous pelecypods of the genus *Inoceramus*, several species of the ammonite genera *Hoploscaphites* and *Baculites*, many different genera and species of smaller pelecypods and gastropods, and rare echinoids. Some of the limestone concretions near the top of the dark exposures of Pierre Shale consist almost entirely of *Inoceramus*. Careful breaking of the concretions may uncover excellent specimens of mollusks, many with the original mother of pearl shell still intact.

Periodically, septarian concretions are found which contain unusual and attractive deposits of calcite and barite crystals. Lying free on the mounds of gray bentonite which occur throughout the area are abundant "fishtail twin" crystals of selenite, and less common gray nodules composed of radiating barite crystals.

Concretions which have washed down from higher levels litter the creek bottoms and often good fossils can be found here. Large pieces of agatized wood frequent the gravels of the creek bottoms, but their source is uncertain. It is certain that they do not weather from the marine Pierre Shale but may originate in the younger Tertiary deposits nearby.

Exposures of the Cretaceous Fox Hills and Hell Creek Formations directly to the east and west of the Pierre Shale outcrops along Cedar Creek are recognized by the presence of light-colored sandstones and greenish-gray shales. These rock units contain fossils similar to those found in the Makoshika State Park area described earlier. They also contain some unusual reddish sandstone concretions which occur as single spheres or groups of spheres. These make interesting additions to a rock collection and are found in gullies and ravines where they have weathered from the rock. Some exposures of the Fox Hills Sandstone just above the outcrops of Pierre Shale will provide specimens of a very unusual fossil. They are rust-colored, cylindrical in shape, about one inch across, and vary in length up to about one foot. They are commonly referred to as "petrified corncobs" probably in reference to their bumpy exterior and general appearance, but they are actually the fossil casts of shrimp burrows.

Much of the land here is public, but portions of it are privately owned. The BLM maps listed should help in determining the status of the land you are interested in exploring. A noticeable occurrence of oil pumping units is apparent as one drives in the Cedar Creek area. A warp in the earth's crust known as the Cedar Creek Anticline is responsible for their presence and large quantities of oil and gas have been obtained here over the past several decades. This geologic structure continues southeast to Baker and fossils can be found in outcrops of the various Cretaceous and Tertiary rocks exposed along its entire length.

The Cedar Creek area can be easily reached by driving south on Merrill Avenue (Marsh Road) from Glendive for about ten miles. The road is paved to the first exposures of Pierre Shale, and then continues as a maintained gravel road to Cedar Creek. The roads and trails in the oil field farther to the south and southeast along Cedar Creek are normally not maintained and can become treacherous when wet, so weather conditions should be considered when planning to enter.

Access Information: Private land, BLM land.

Useful Maps: BLM Public Lands in Montana maps; 20 *Savage*, and 30 *Fallon*.
U.S. Geological Survey *Glendive, Hoyt,* and *Upper Magpie Reservoir* Quadrangles, Montana; 7.5 Minute Series, Topographic scale 1:24,000

Specific References: Bishop, G.S. *Geology, Stratigraphy, and Biostratigraphy of the North End of Cedar Creek Anticline, Dawson County, Montana.* Montana Bureau of Mines and Geology Special Publication 61, 1973.

Brown, R. W. *Fossil Plants from the Colgate Member of the Fox Hills Sandstone and Adjacent Strata.* U.S. Geological Survey Professional Paper 189-I, 1939.

Brown, R. W. *Paleocene Flora of the Rocky Mountains and Great Plains.* U.S. Geological Survey Professional Paper 375, 1962.

Hiatt, R. W. *Makoshika State Park,* Glendive Montana: R. W. Hiatt and Glendive Women's Club, Publishers, 1974.

Taylor, O. J. *Ground-Water Resources along Cedar Creek Anticline in Eastern Montana.* Montana Bureau of Mines and Geology Memoir 40, 1965.

Fort Peck Reservoir Area

During the late 1800's and early 1900's the Missouri River was a transportation route to the wilderness regions of the west. Several large paddle-wheel boats regularly made their way between Fort Benton and the larger cities of Omaha and St. Louis. Traders, trappers, and settlers began to infiltrate the area and it was inevitable that the U.S. Army was brought into the region to protect these persevering people.

Fort Peck itself was never a military post, however. It was used primarily as a source of materials and services for the early trappers and traders. The stockade was initially situated very close to the river and eventually erosion by the river destroyed the ledge upon which the fort was built. The initial site presently lies beneath the waters of the tremendous reservoir created by Fort Peck Dam, completed in 1937.

Since Fort Peck is situated close to U.S. Highway 2, tourists often stop to visit one of the largest earth-filled dams in the world. They are generally amazed because, as seen from downstream or from the community of Fort Peck, the dam is nothing more than a straight, gentle slope.

Powerhouse Number One on the northeast edge of the dam houses a fine display of fossils. This display is described in more detail later in the book. The fossils, for the most part, were collected in close proximity to Fort Peck, but a collector's paradise it is not, at least for the rock hobbyist. The shoreline and hills adjacent to Fort Peck Reservoir are located within the boundaries of the C.M. Russell National Wildlife Refuge and, as indicated earlier, federal regulations prohibit the collecting of fossils for hobby purposes on these lands.

The Fort Peck Reservoir area provides some of the best exposures of the Cretaceous Bearpaw Shale, Judith River, and Hell Creek formations to be found in the state. The most impressive fossils which have been collected from these rocks are the remains of dinosaurs.

Charles Sternberg and Edward Cope explored the badlands of the Judith River Formation in the western part of the Fort Peck Reservoir area during the late 1800's and discovered many dinosaurs. Most were the "duckbilled" varieties, but the addition of many new species to eastern U.S. museums continued to fuel the personal conlict that existed between Cope and his paleontological adversary, Othniel Marsh. The rivalry that was shared by these two "scientists" is well documented in many books. One of these is *The Bone Hunters*, by Url Lanham, and those who are interested in the historical aspect of paleontology will find the reading most enjoyable.

The word "hell" is often used to describe the bleakness and desolation of a region like the area south of Fort Peck Reservoir near Jordan. Geologists indicate that this region, now known as Hell Creek, did not always appear as it does today. The layers of sedimentary rock exposed here reveal not only evidence of a much milder climate but also the existence of many different and unusual plants and animals.

In the early 1900's Barnum Brown, a paleontologist for the American Museum of Natural History, discovered in the 65 million year old sediments of the Hell Creek Formation the skeletal remains of a remarkable creature. A large skull with teeth up to six inches long indicates that the animal was a carnivore and dominated other creatures which shared its habitat. Although only a few nearly complete skeletons and several skulls make up all we know of it, *Tyrannosaurus rex* has come to epitomize the dinosaur.

A nearly complete skeleton of *Tyrannosaurus rex* found by a local rockhound was recently excavated by paleontologists from the Museum of the Rockies in Bozeman. The find is one of extreme importance because the specimen is relatively intact. It is, in fact, the first specimen to provide definite information about the forelimbs. The speciment is currently being prepared, while on display, at the Museum of the Rockies.

Tyrannosaurus is not the only dinosaur to be collected from the Hell Creek sediments. Skulls of the armored, three-horned dinosaur *Triceratops*, are frequently found as well as the remains of *Hadrosaurs* and the rare *Ankylosaurs*.

The sediments of the Hell Creek Formation southeast of the Fort peck Reservoir have produced more than just dinosaurs. Numerous skeletal remains of

Makoshika State Park south of Glendive.

Badlands of the Cretaceous Hell Creek Formation along Hell Creek north of Jordan. Formation is a source of dinosaur remains such as Tyrannosaurus rex.

tiny mammals have been collected from several badlands areas. They, in fact, are being studied perhaps more intensely than are the dinosaurs of this area at the present. Finds such as these contribute a great deal to the scientific study of the Mesozoic-Tertiary boundary conflict that presently exists in the western interior of North America. Scientists have had difficulty in determining where rocks of Cretaceous age end and rocks of Paleocene age begin because of the few fossils which are found in these layers.

Access Information: National Wildlife Refuge (No hobby collecting!)
Useful Maps: BLM Public Lands in Montana maps: 16 *Breaks,* 17 *UL Bend,* and 18 *Haxby.*
U.S. Geological Survey *Fort Peck* Quadrangle, Montana; 7.5 Minute Series, Topographic, scale 1:24,000.
U.S. Geological Survey *Maloney Hill* Quadrangle, Montana; 15 Minutes Series, Topographic, scale 1:62,500.
Specific References:
Colton, R.B., and Bateman, A. F., Jr. *Geologic and Structure Contour Map of the Fort Peck Indian Reservation and Vicinity, Montana.* U.S. Geological Survey Miscellaneous Geologic Investigations Map L-225, 1956.
Conlin, D.G., and Burnett, G. W. "The Bones of Purgatory," *Montana Outdoors,* Vol. II, No. 5, 1980, pp. 24-26.
Hager, M. W. "Strange Beasts in Our Backyard," *Montana Outdoors,* Vol. II, No. 5, 1980, pp. 2-5.

Jensen, F. S., and Varnes, H. D. *Geology of the Fort Peck Area, Garfield, McCone, and Valley Counties, Montana.* U.S. Geological Survey Professional Paper, 414-F, 1964.

Sahni, Ashok. *The Vertebrate Fauna of the Judith River Formation, Montana.* Bulletin of the American Museum of Natural History, Vol. 147, Art. 6, 1972.

Fossils Near Miles City

The Tertiary Fort Union Formation which is so predominant in the eastern part of Montana has been a prolific source of extremely well preserved fossil leaf prints. The leaf prints of hardwood trees such as birch, elm, oak, and maple are most common. Periodically logs, stumps, and limbs of fossilized sequoia trees are found weathering in hillsides. The gravels of some stream bottoms in the region contain relatively large fragments of colorful agatized wood, ideal for rock gardens, but keep in mind the government regulation concerning petrified wood if you are on public land and decide to take any of this material. In some cases, one or two pieces could easily fill the yearly quota.

Most exposures of the Fort Union Formation in highway roadcuts have the potential of producing fine fossil leaf prints if the thin-bedded sandstones and hard shales are carefully split with hammer and chisel. Sometimes the red "clinker" beds will disclose fine delicate impressions of leaves. These red clinker beds represent clays and mudstones which were baked by the natural burning of coal layers underground. The highly baked clays which now outcrop along the crests of hills in the area have the appearance of volcanic rock, and are called "scoria" by local ranchers.

It is difficult to pinpoint any one locality for fossil leaves in the Fort Union Formation since they are fairly common throughout, but one typical locality can be reached by driving about eight miles east of Miles City on U.S. Highway 12. The leaf prints here can be found by splitting the layers of red colored shale. Roadcuts along this same route, or the route between Miles City and Broadus, should produce additional and similar specimens if the rock layers are examined carefully.

More rarely, the sediments of the Fort Union Formation reveal the skeletal remains and teeth of crocodile-like reptiles, turtles, small mammals, and mollusks. Many years ago, this writer had the opportunity to view a most outstanding fossil from this general region. The fossil is that of a relatively complete upper jaw of a crocodile bearing a good number of perfect conical teeth. The jaw is several feet in length and beautifully preserved. It was collected by a geologist when the region was being explored for petroleum and coal sources. The specimen was removed from a channel sandstone unit in the Lebo Member of the Fort Union Formation and was associated with several fragmental remains of turtles and gar fish. The turtle remains include some bones, teeth, and small plates from its shell, while the gar fish remains consist of very dark colored, diamond-shaped scales. These scales are often common in some of these channel sandstone deposits.

The environment which existed in eastern Montana during Lebo time has been interpreted as a low elevation landscape of very low relief, and criss-crossed by numerous stream channels in which lived many varieties of fresh-water animals. The climate was apparently sub-tropical, as evidenced by the fossil crocodile jaw, and therefore not unlike that of the southeastern United States today. With this type of interpretation, one might expect fossils such

FOSSILS NEAR MILES CITY

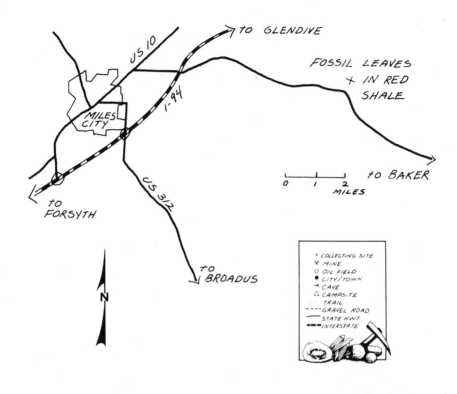

as these to be extremely abundant wherever rock units such as these occur. However, the exposures of channel sandstones are not overly common, nor are they always well exposed. Considerable searching and just plain luck are necessary to uncover an exotic specimen like the crocodile mentioned earlier.

Access Information: Private land.
Useful Maps: BLM Public Lands in Montana map: 29 *Custer.*
U.S. Geological Survey *Miles City, Government Hill,* and *The Knob* Quadrangles, Montana; 7.5 Minute Series, Topographic, scale 1:24,000.
Specific References:

Brown, R. W. *Paleocene Flora of the Rocky Mountains and Great Plains.* U.S. Geological Survey Professional Paper 375, 1962.
Garrett, H. L. *Fossil Slump Features of the Tertiary Paleocene Fort Union,* Billings Geological Society Special Papers, 1963.
Tidwell, W. D. *Common Fossil Plants of Western North America.* Provo, Utah: Brigham Young University Press, 197 pp., 1975.
Yen, Teng-Chien. *Paleocene Fresh-Water Mollusks from Southern Montana.* U.S. Geological Survey Professional Papers 214-C, 1948.

Colstrip

Perhaps one of man's most important concerns at this time is the rapidly dwindling reserves of fossil fuels and the continuing need for energy. The area around Colstrip is infamous for its large deposits of low sulfur coal, which occur as relatively thick seams in the Tertiary Fort Union Formation and have been strip-mined for many years.

Mining of the predominantly sub-bituminous coal began in 1923 and continued intermittently up to 1968 when Western Energy Company, a subsidiary of Montana Power Company, resumed mining activity on a full time basis. Coal production is about 12 million tons per year and the mining operation is truly spectacular. The unique workings of the huge dragline, in particular its movement across the landscape, are a tribute to man's technology, but the large ore trucks moving to and fro make the area very hazardous. The active mining areas where trucks are hauling coal should be avoided, unless on an official guided tour.

Exposures of the Fort Union Formation in the area contain rock layers with well preserved fossil leaf prints, similar to those found near Miles City. Several abandoned "scoria" pits and mine tailings can be found near Colstrip, and these would be the best places to search for fossils. Be sure to check locally, however, to avoid trespassing on private land. Caution should also be exercised when examining these pits and tailings since they are often inhabited by rattlesnakes. Rocks should be turned over with a rock hammer or some extension of your own arm: black widow spiders take up residence underneath.

Additional information about tours or rock collecting around Colstrip may be obtained at the MPC field office in Colstrip.

Huge dragline removes rock lying above coal deposits. Colstrip, Montana.

Access Information: Private land, patented and unpatented mining claims.
Useful Maps: BLM Public Lands in Montana map: 38 *Tongue.*
U.S. Geological Survey *Colstrip East, Colstrip SE, Colstrip SW, and Colstrip West* Quadrangles, Montana; 7.5 Minute Series, Topographic, scale 1:24,000.
Specific References:

Brown, R. W. *Paleocene Flora of the Rocky Mountains and Great Plains.* U.S. Geological Survey Professional Paper 375, 1962.

Cole, G. A., Matson, R. E., and Pederson, R. J. *Montana Coal.* Montana Bureau of Mines and Geology Special Publication 83, 1980.

Tidwell, W. D. *Common Fossil Plants of Western North America.* Provo, Utah: Brigham Young University Press, 197 pp., 1975.

Little Rocky Mountains Area

Placer gold was discovered here in 1884, but ten years of continuous placer operations took place before the lode deposits containing the gold were mined. Apparently, the alluvial deposits in which the gold was first discovered are very extensive, but the quantity of water needed to work these deposits is not available. Lode deposits have since provided the major amounts of recoverable gold in the district.

The unusual occurrence of this small rugged mountain mass in the plains of northern Montana is attributed to volcanism. The Little Rockies are basically interpreted as a laccolithic structure, that is, an area domed upward as a result of molten magma intruding between sedimentary rock layers and pushing them from below. A later period of erosion has exposed the igneous rock core and the metalliferous veins it contains. The metals of interest here are gold and silver, but various sulfide minerals should occur on the dumps if they are accessible.

Several of the mines near Zortman and Landusky have been reactivated and therefore access to dumps and tailings here is doubtful. The Landusky Mining Company has recently provided passes which will allow visitors to participate in a guided tour of mining operations.

Paleozoic and Mesozoic rock layers are turned up sharply along the margins of the Little Rockies, and exposures of various fossiliferous formations often occur in these areas. Limestones of the Mississippian Mission Canyon and Lodgepole Formations have been reported to produce some very fine fossils in this region. The marine Jurassic shales here continue to yield relatively common specimens of the oyster *Gryphaea*, the belemnite *Pachyteuthis*, the starshaped crinoid columnals of *Pentacrinus*, as well as less common species of ammonites and brachiopods.

Since many roads lead into the Little Rockies, road cuts in the marginal areas of the mountains should be thoroughly examined for outcrops of fossiliferous rock.

Access Information: Private land, BLM land, patented and unpatented mining claims.
Useful Maps: BLM Public Lands in Montana maps: 6 *Belknap* and 16 *Breaks.*
U.S. Geological Survey *Zortman* Quadrangle, Montana; 7.5 Minute Series, Topographic, scale 1:24,000.

LITTLE ROCKY MOUNTAINS AREA

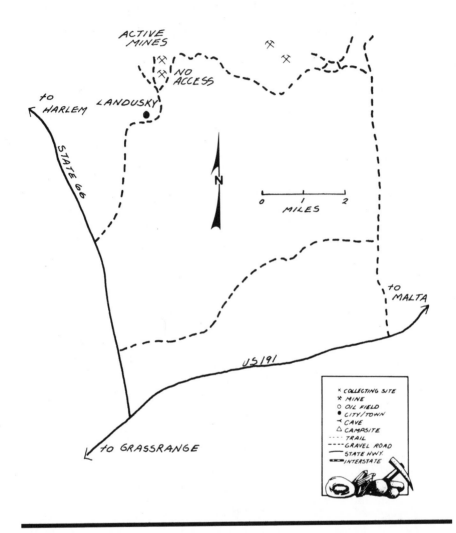

Specific References:
Bryant, F. B. *History and Development of the Landusky Mining District, Little Rocky Mountains, Montana.* Billings Geological Society 4th Annual Field Conference Guidebook, pp. 161-163, 1953.

Corry, A. V. *Some Gold Deposits of Broadwater, Beaverhead, Phillips and Fergus Counties, Montana.* Montana Bureau of Mines and Geology Memoir 10, 1933.

Dyson, J. L. *Ruby Gulch Gold Mining District, Little Rocky Mountains, Montana.* Billings Geological Society 4th Annual Field Conference Guidebook, pp. 164-169, 1953.

Emmons, W. H. *Gold Deposits of the Little Rocky Mountains, Montana.* U.S. Geological Survey Bulletin 340, 1908.

Knechtel, M. M. *Stratigraphy of the Little Rocky Mountains and Encircling Foothills, Montana.* U.S. Geological Survey Bulletin 1072-N, 1959.

MONTANA "DIAMONDS" NORTH OF LEWISTOWN

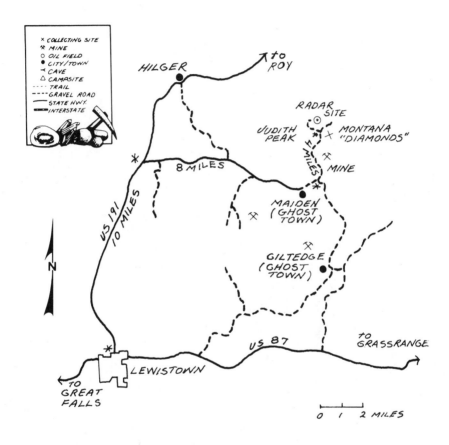

Montana "Diamonds" North of Lewistown

Found high on a peak of the Judith Mountains north of Lewistown is one of the more unique mineral collecting areas in the state. Small doubly terminated crystals of quartz, often referred to as Montana or black "diamonds," whether from the porphyritic rock containing them and are sought after by mineral collectors primarily because of their extremely uniform shape. Although interesting and very abundant, they lack the quality of the famed Herkimer "diamonds" of New York and New Jersey. The crystals are not clear, but are generally a very dark smoky and opaque variety of quartz. Sizes range from about one-fourth inch to an inch in diameter. The crystals have also been used as jewelry items by some rockhounds because of their perfect symmetrical form.

The area is reached by driving about ten miles north of Lewistown on U.S. Highway 191 to the Maiden road, where a right turn is required. About eight miles of paved road leads eastward to the old mining camp of Maiden. The town is now pretty much in ruins, but the sites of the different buildings have been marked with signs, and by walking among the ruins one can get a dim glimpse of the past. An additional four miles on a good but sometimes steep and winding gravel road will take one to the outcrops of the quartz porphyry.

The porphyry is highly weathered, and the doubly terminated crystals are lying free in the soil and weathered rock in the large road cuts near the summit of the peak. The main collecting area cannot be missed because of its light color and the fact that it has apparently been "dug into" quite a bit. Several other road cuts nearby will produce good crystals but they are certainly not as common as they are at the main collecting site. The crystals of dark quartz are easily seen in the solid rock of which the road cut is composed, but they normally cannot be removed from the unweathered rock without being broken. The best crystals are those which have weathered naturally from the rock, but be selective because most are not of high quality. Making up a good portion of the rock enclosing the quartz phenocrysts are light-colored, terminated feldspar crystals. Although most are small, some attain a length of about 3/8 inch and could possibly make attractive micromounts. Look for these in the soil and weathered rock which contain the quartz crystals. The texture of the rock containing the quartz and feldspar crystals demonstrates its plutonic or intrusive nature.

In some of the adjacent roadcuts above and below the major Montana "diamond" locality there is a much finer-grained rock which periodically contains veins of dark smoky quartz. On occasion, the veins have small cavities lined with small but nicely terminated black quartz crystals. Sometimes these crystals break loose from the walls of the cavities and can be found loose in the dirt on the face of a road cut. Some small groups of crystals, ideal for thumbnail collections, have been found.The summit of the peak, about .5 mile beyond the main collecting area for the Montana "diamonds," was at one time the site of a U.S. Air Force radar station. The buildings have been abandoned and most have been vandalized. The view from the old radar site is well worth the short drive from the collecting sites. On a clear day, most of the nearby mountain systems can be viewed, as well as several interesting geologic features on the prairies to the east.

If you are a weekend gold prospector, you might want to try your luck at panning the gravels of the many small streams in the valleys below the peaks in the vicinity of Maiden. Be sure, however, that you are on BLM land and

Spectacular scenery dominates much of western Montana.

not private or claimed property. Some of the small mines in the area are still being explored and developed by small mining enterprises.

Access Information: BLM land, state land, and private land.

Useful Maps: BLM Public Lands in Montana map: 15 *Judith.* U.S. Geological Survey *Lewistown and Judith Peaks* Quadrangles, Montana; 15 Minute Series, Topographic scale 6:62,500.

Specific References: Eichorn, L. C. "Montana Diamonds," *Gems and Minerals,* No. 409, 1971, p. 23.

Yogo Gulch

Of the known sapphire localities, one of the more famous is in central Montana about forty-five miles southwest of Lewistown, in the Little Belt Mountains. The deep "cornflower" blue color of the sapphires found here rivals even that of the Ceylon varieties.

YOGO GULCH

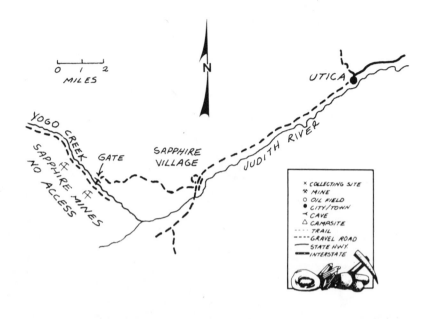

Yogo Gulch was originally a source of placer gold, and it was strictly by chance that the Yogo sapphire was discovered. Because of their relatively high density, the unusual blue stones were common in the gold-bearing stream gravels. Curiosity resulted in an evaluation of the stones, and then placer operations were begun to retrieve sapphires along with gold. These operations continued up to the investigation and eventual mining of a large, four-mile-long igneous dike containing the sapphires. Both British and American mining enterprises have been involved in the sporadic operations in Yogo Gulch with the British operations perhaps being more pronounced until the present.

Inaccessible to collectors, the mine is currently being developed by Intergem Incorporated of Colorado, and there is a great deal of confidence that gems will continue to be produced from this famous area for some time to come. Since collecting at the mine is not allowed, rough Yogo sapphires are not easily acquired by those who prefer to facet their own gemstones. Finished Yogo sapphire jewelry, on the other hand, because of its popularity, is sold in just about every jewelry store in Montana, as well as many major ones across the nation.

The current owners have proposed a new name for the Yogo sapphire— "The Royal American." This of course may be their prerogative, but those who have been familiar with this gemstone over many decades will most certainly continue to refer to it as "The Yogo".

The colorful history of Yogo Gulch is well documented in several issues of various popular rockhound magazines. The history is also generalized in the U.S. Geological Survey publication on corundum by S. E. Clabaugh. Fairly recently, a real estate promotion initiated the beginning of Sapphire Village, a collection of small lots where buyers could build summer homes and pan or screen for the famed Yogo sapphire on their own property. The geomorphology and geology of the lot area is such that accumulations of sapphires there may be minimal.

Access Information: Private land, patented and unpatented mining claims; NO ACCESS!

Useful Maps: BLM Public Lands in Montana map: 24 *Castles*. U.S Geological Survey *Bandbox Mtn., Browns Canyon, Indian Hill, Red Hill, Utica,* and *Woodhurst Mtn.* Quadrangles, Montana; 7.5 Minute Series, Topographic, scale 1:24,000.

Specific References: Blodgett, M. M. "Timeless Land of the Yogo Sapphire," *Lapidary Journal,* Vol. 35, No. 2, 1981, pp. 560-569, May, 1981.

Clabaugh, S. E. *Corundum Deposits of Montana.* U.S. Geological Survey Bulletin 983, pp. 6-34, 1952.

Howard, D. L. "No Ghosts at Yogo," *Lapidary Journal,* Vol. 16, Nos. 1 and 2, April and May, 1962.

Johnson, B. J. "Montana's Famed Yogo Gulch," *Gems and Minerals,* No.437, pp. 30-31, March, 1974.

Leiper, Hugh, "Five Miles of Sapphires," *Lapidary Journal,* Vol. 22, No. 10, pp. 1278-1286, January, 1969.

Yaras, Herman. "Precious Yogo Sapphires Will Again Gleam Among The World's Precious Jewels," *Lapidary Journal,* Vol. 23, No. 1, pp. 178-180, April, 1969.

Big Snowy Mountains South of Lewistown

To describe exactly where fossils can be found in the Big Snowy Mountains would be a difficult task for many reasons. Fossils of ages ranging from Early Paleozoic to Mesozoic can be found throughout the range where outcrops of these rocks occur. Many roads lead into the mountains and so one needs only to find a good outcrop and begin searching. A few specific localities are mentioned here, but a general knowledge of the various rock strata will help in finding fossils at most outcrops.

The Mississippian Madison Limestone is well exposed, and wherever it is encountered fossils are more than likely. The fossils are marine types and consist of many species of brachiopods, corals, and crinoids. Most frequently, the specimens are preserved in hard, massive limestone and can only be collected if a large portion of the limestone containing them is also taken. Relatively complete crinoids have been found in some of the thin-bedded limestones which occur in the Madison Formation. These, however, are difficult to find and are obviously highly prized.

The foothills of the range consist of upturned layers of Mesozoic rocks and marine fossils such as the belemnite *Pachyteuthis,* the oyster *Gryphaea,* and the star-shaped columnals of the crinoid *Pentacrinus* can be found. The Jurassic shales appear to be the best fossil producing rocks in the Mesozoic sequence here, but good exposures of it are not common.

The road leading to Crystal Lake, a popular camping area in the northwestern part of the Big Snowy Mountains, passes through upturned units of Paleozoic rocks and provides easy access to varying ages of rocks. A search of the road cuts and cliffs as this road is traversed reveals the fossiliferous nature of many of the beds.

The Red Hill Road provides access to the eastern part of the range. Here roadcuts expose rocks of Paleozoic and Mesozoic age, providing good potential for the collecting of fossils. The Red Hill Road leads south of the Heath railroad siding and passes through mostly private land.

A fairly recent discovery of fossil sharks and other fish—remarkably preserved—was made in the vicinity of Bear Gulch on the eastern side of the Snowy Mountains. The fossils occur in a thin-bedded limestone of apparent Pennsylvanian age, which has been quarried for several years. This quarry has been worked by professional paleontologists during the summer months of the past several decades, and new discoveries continue to be made. This is definitely a locality in which the amateur should not collect since important information concerning the fauna which existed here during the Pennsylvanian Period could be destroyed by improper collecting techniques. Arrangements might be made with the various paleontological teams investigating the area to visit and observe them as they excavate the fossils.

The fossils which have been collected here represent a wide variety of sharks and several orders of fish. The preservation of the fossils is incredible because of the extremely fine-grained texture of the rock containing them and the apparent conditions under which the animals lived, died, and were buried. The absence of scavengers where the burial of the animals took place may explain the relative abundance and completeness of the finds.

A discovery of particular interest was made at the quarry in the late 1960s by a professor from the University of Montana. The specimens may represent the remains of the animal from which the tiny teeth-like fossils called conodonts originate. Studies are still being conducted and some disagreement apparently exists concerning the exact identity of this fossil, but it at least represents a step towards solving one of the major paleontological mysteries which presently exist.

Access Information: Private land, National Forest Service land.
Useful Maps: BLM Public Lands in Montana map: 25 *Snowy.*
USDA Forest Service Forest Visitors Map; Lewis and Clark National Forest, Jefferson Division, Montana.
U.S. Geological Survey *Alaska Bench, Castle Butte, Crystal Lake, Forest Grove, Half Moon Canyon, Heath, Jump Off Peak, Loco Ridge, Moore SW, South Bench,* and *West Fork Beaver Creek* Quadrangles, Montana; 7.5 Minute Series, Topographic, scale 1:24,000.
U.S. Geological Survey, *Lewistown* and *Judith Peak* Quadrangles, Mon-tana; 15 Minute Series, Topographic, scale 1:62,500.
Specific References:
Berg, R. B. *Building Stone in Montana.* Montana Bureau of Mines and Geology Bulletin 94, p. 17, 1974.
Easton, W. H. *Carboniferous Formations and Faunas of Central Montana.* U.S. Geological Survey Professional Paper 348, 1962.
Melton, W. G. *The Bear Gulch Limestone and the First Conodont Bearing Animals.* Montana Geological Society 21st Annual Geological Conference Guidebook, Crazy Mountains Basin, pp. 66-68, 1972.

Fossils North of Roundup

About twenty-four miles north of Roundup several rock outcrops in roadcuts along U.S. Highway 87 can produce some interesting fossils. The first locality is encountered about three miles north of the Route 244 junction to Winnett. Here, as Highway 87 descends into the valley of Flat Willow Creek, several roadcuts in exposures of the Cretaceous Colorado Shale are found. The Mosby Sandstone Member is well exposed in the northern most

FOSSILS NORTH OF ROUNDUP

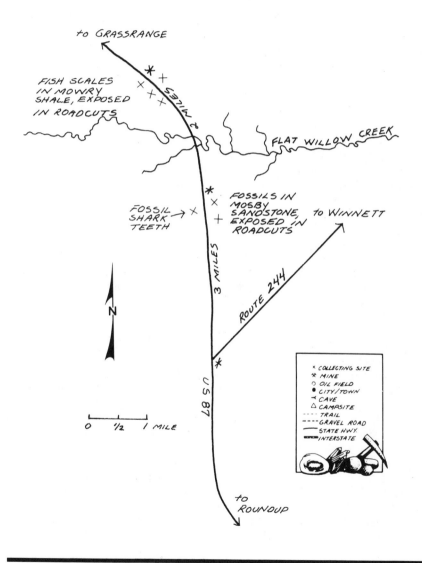

roadcut on the east side of the highway. Specimens of the fossil oyster *Gryphaea* can be picked up on the surface of the roadcut while, here and there, sandy concretions containing a fair abundance of fossil snails (mostly *Pseudomelania hendricksoni* (Henderson) are found. Some of the adjacent roadcuts contain limestone concretions with attractive white and brown calcite crystals. Crystals of selenite are abundant on the surface of all of the road cuts. On the west side of the highway, directly across from the Mosby Sandstone outcrops, is a relatively high roadcut. The light colored shale beds near the top have been reported to contain fossil shark teeth of several genera and species *(Isurus, Squalicorax,* and *Ptychodus)* but they are not at all common and diligent searching is required to find them.

About two miles further north along U.S. 87 (five miles north of the Route 244 junction to Winnett) are some low road cuts on both sides of the highway exposing the Cretaceous Mowry Shale. By splitting the light colored, thin bedded layers, one can find abundant fish scales and assorted fish remains. No complete fish skeletons have yet been found in rocks such as these, but the extreme abundance of fossil scales within certain bedding planes is quite interesting in itself. The scales appear as black to brown spots, 1/8 inch to 1/4 inch across, dotting the surface of an exposed shale layer. Some magnification (10X hand lens) will reveal the concentric ring pattern on the surface of the scales. Periodically, fish teeth and small vertebrae are found.

Access Information: Highway right of way, adjacent private land.
Useful Maps: BLM Public Lands in Montana map: 26 *Roundup.* U.S. Geological Survey *Roundup* NL 12-6, scale 1:250,000.
Specific References: Johnson, W. D., Jr., and Smith H. R. *Geology of the Winnett-Mosby Area, Petroleum, Garfield, Rosebud, and Fergus Counties, Montana.* U.S. Geological Survey Bulletin 1149, 1964.

Fossils at Yellow Water Reservoir

Yellow Water Reservoir is reached by driving 7.5 miles south of Winnett on Route 244 and then 5.5 miles due west on a gravel and dirt road. This road should not be attempted when it is wet, since it becomes slippery and hazardous.

A conspicuous sandstone ledge and cuesta parallels the southern shoreline of the reservoir for some distance. The ledge is formed in the Mosby Sandstone Member of the Cretaceous Colorado Shale, and in spots is very fossiliferous. Sand concretions are frequently found which contain abundant snails (*Pseudomelania hendricksoni* (Henderson), *Lunatia* sp., and *Gyrodes* sp.), some oysters (*Gryphaea* sp. and *Exogyra* sp.), and occasional specimens of the relatively large ammonites (*Dunveganoceras* sp. and *Metoicoceras* sp.). Extremely nice specimens of these ammonites from this locality have been placed in private collections as well as the U.S. Geological Survey collection, but apparently they are becoming increasingly difficult to find.

To the south and north of the reservoir, outcrops of the Upper Mosby Sandstone and the Basal Carlile Member of the Colorado Shale are exposed. Fossils seem to be scarce in these beds, but interesting specimens have been found. Some fossil shark teeth have been reported from outcrops south of the reservoir, but the exact source of them is uncertain.

FOSSILS AT YELLOW WATER RESERVOIR S.W. OF WINNETT

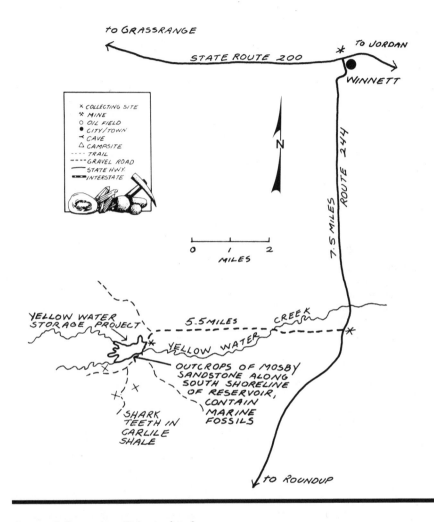

Access Information: Private land.

Useful Maps: BLM Public Lands in Montana map: 26 *Roundup.*

U.S. Geological Survey *Roundup* NL 12-6, scale 1:250,000.

Specific References: Cobban, W. A. *Cenomanian Ammonite Fauna from the Mosby Sandstone of Central Montana.* U.S. Geological Survey Professional Paper 243-D, 1953.

Johnson, W. D. Jr., and Smith, H. R. *Geology of the Winnett-Mosby Area, Petroleum, Garfield, Rosebud, and Fergus Counties, Montana.* U.S. Geological Survey Bulletin 1149, 1964.

Fossils Near Melstone and Ingomar

Broad expanses of the Late Cretaceous Bearpaw Shale of marine origin occur in the area between Melstone and Vananda along U.S. Highway 12. There is potential here for collecting fine fossils, but exposures along the highway itself are very limited. One must leave the highway and explore the ravines and hills, all of which occur on private land.

Several relatively small geological structures in the area near Melstone and Sumatra have been exploited for petroleum. Numerous small roads have been constructed, but the apparent easy access and lack of gates or fences should not be misconstrued. Private land prevails here and access for collecting must be approved by the land owner.

Classic specimens of several genera and species of ammonites have been collected in this region. The genera include *Placenticeras, Rhaeboceras, Didymoceras, Hoploscaphites, Exiteloceras, Solenoceras,* and many species of *Baculites,* which is perhaps the most common fossil type found here. Assorted species of pelecypods and gastropods with periodic occurrences of fossil lobsters represent some of the other fossil types found here.

Exposures in the banks of the Musselshell River and hills adjacent to many intermittent streams are places to look for specimens. The fossils are contained in limestone concretions and are exposed when the concretions are broken. Care must be taken in doing this, however, so that the entombed fossil is not damaged.

It is difficult to pinpoint specific locations in which fossils can be found. One needs to located exposed shale layers and trace them while sampling concretions within that layer. One should also watch for the remains of fossil vertebrates, mostly fragmental remains (ribs, vertebrae, etc.) of *Mosasaurs.* Keep in mind that special techniques are required for excavating complete vertebrate remains from rock.

With the exception of a small syncline between Sumatra and Ingomar which exposes younger rocks (such as the Fox Hills Sandstone and Hell Creek Formation) the Bearpaw Shale remains pretty much uninterrupted between Melstone and Vananda.

Access Information: Private land.
Useful Maps: BLM Public Lands in Montana map: 27 *Sumatra.*
U.S. Geological Survey *Ahles, Grebe Ranch, Cuthridge Ranch, Hecker Ranch, Ingomar East, Ingomar West, Melstone NE, Sumatra, Thebes, Vananda,* and *Zempel Lake* Quadrangles, Montana; 7.5 Minute Series, Topographic, scale 1:24,000.
Specific References: Smith, H. R. *Geology of the Melstone-Sumatra Area in Central Montana.* U.S. Geological Survey Oil and Gas Investigations Map OM-211, 1962.

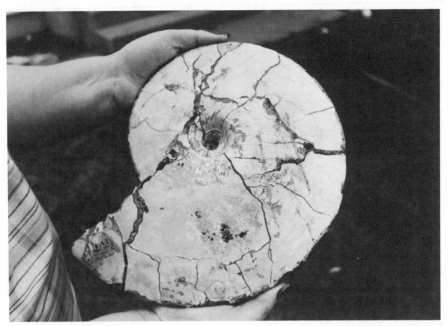

Specimen of the ammonite Placenticeras meeki *Boehm from the Bearpaw Shale of Central Montana.*

FOSSILS NEAR MELSTONE AND INGOMAR

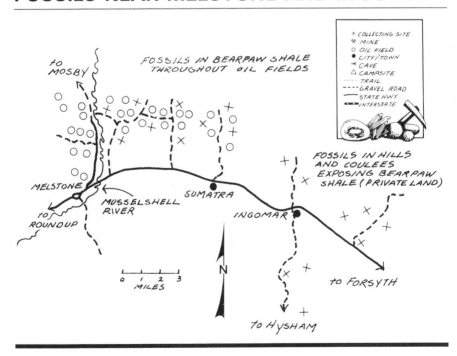

FOSSILS SOUTH OF ROUNDUP

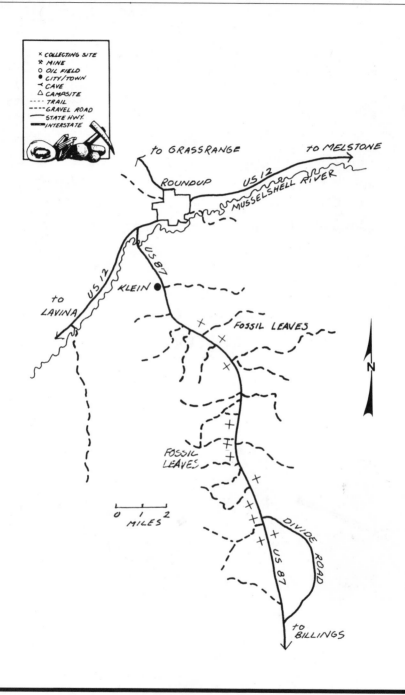

Rod Charlton of Billings wonders if these beds might yield some fine fossil leaf prints.

Fossils South of Roundup

Roundup is situated on the north end of the relatively large Bull Mountain Syncline. Although the area is somewhat high topographically, the structure is essentially a down-warped one in which rocks of Tertiary age are exposed. The primary strata here are sandstones and shales belonging to the Tongue River Member of the Fort Union Formation. There are numerous coal seams, presently mined on a small scale mainly for local consumption.

The shales and thin-bedded sandstone units within the Tongue River Member will frequently produce beautifully preserved fossil leaf prints. Specific localities where the prints can be collected are difficult to describe and many are on private land where access is questionable. The writer has obtained some relatively good specimens of various species (mostly elm, oak, birch, etc.) by searching road cuts, the most accessible being those south of Roundup for a distance of about fourteen miles along U.S. Highway 87. A rock hammer and a set of chisels would be useful here in splitting the rock layers. The road cuts along the highway are very steep and extreme caution is advised if you plan to climb them. Be sure that you do not allow rocks to fall from the road cuts on to the highway.

Access Information: Highway right of way, private land.
Useful Maps: BLM Public Lands in Montana map: 26 *Roundup*.
U.S. Geological Survey *Roundup NL* 12-6, scale 1:250,000.
Specific References:
Brown, R. W. *Paleocene Flora of the Rocky Mountains and Great Plains.* U.S. Geological Survey Professional Paper 375.
Tidwell, W. D. *Common Fossil Plants of Western North America.* Provo, Utah: Brigham Young University Press, 197 pp. 1975.

Fossil oysters Crassostrea subtrigonalis *(Evans and Shumard) in sandstone. South of Lavina; Cretaceous Judith River Formation.*

Fossils Near Lavina

An interesting outcrop of the Cretaceous Judith River Formation can be viewed just south of Lavina. To find it, drive south of Lavina on Route 3 for one mile, then turn east on a gravel road and drive .5 mile. The outcrop will be to your right at the top of the hill.

The locality is one of geological interest. The road cut displays several units of lignite coal interbedded with sandstone, shale, and layers of oysters. The presence of the fossil oysters is evidence that the plant material which accumulated to form the thin units of lignite was situated in a near-shore environment. This kind of evidence is apparent at many coal deposits in the western interior region. The oysters here belong to a single genus and species, *Crassostrea subtrigonalis* (Evans and Shumard), and represent, more or less, the only fossil form other than the lignite deposits found in the road cut. Occasionally some pieces of petrified wood are found in adjacent strata. Outcrops of Cretaceous Bearpaw Shale farther south have yielded some fine ammonites and other marine fossils, but that area has been collected extensively and it is doubtful that even if access to those exposures is gained, much can be found.

Several road cuts along the north side of U.S. Highway 12 about 9.7 miles west of Lavina expose the Judith River Formation and here, too, the fossil oyster *Crassostrea subtrigonalis* can be found in great abundance. The beds of oysters alternate with beds of sandstone, lignite, and shale suggesting a continually changing environment. Diastrophic processes must certainly have been at work in this region in the geologic past, causing the land to rise and fall at frequent intervals.

Access Information: Private land.
Useful Maps: BLM Public Lands in Montana map: 26 *Roundup*.
U.S. Geological Survey *Belmont* and *Lavina* Quadrangles, Montana; 7.5 Minute
    Series, Topographic, scale 1:24,000.
Specific References: None.

FOSSILS NEAR LAVINA

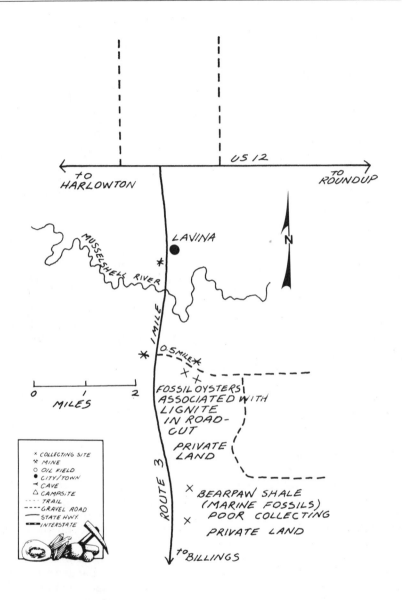

US 12

to HARLOWTON

to ROUNDUP

N

LAVINA

MUSSELSHELL RIVER

1 MILE

0.5 MILE

0   1   2
MILES

FOSSIL OYSTERS
ASSOCIATED WITH
LIGNITE
IN ROAD-
CUT

PRIVATE
LAND

ROUTE 3

BEARPAW SHALE
(MARINE FOSSILS)
POOR COLLECTING

PRIVATE LAND

to BILLINGS

× COLLECTING SITE
✶ MINE
○ OIL FIELD
● CITY/TOWN
◄ CAVE
△ CAMPSITE
···· TRAIL
---- GRAVEL ROAD
―― STATE HWY.
━━ INTERSTATE

The Billings Area

At Billings one cannot help but notice the conspicuous buff-colored cliffs which border the city on the north and east sides. These cliffs are made up of several rock units within the Late Cretaceous Eagle Sandstone Formation. Stratigraphic and sedimentologic investigations indicate that these sandstones were deposited as beaches and off-shore bars on the fluctuating western margin of an inland sea. One would therefore expect to find abundant fossil shells much like one would find modern shells along a present-day sandy beach. But fossil occurrences within the Eagle Sandstone around Billings are scattered and very localized. Even when found, they are, for the most part, poorly preserved.

Some Eagle Sandstone units do produce good fossils. The writer has a fine specimen of a large nautiloid which was collected from the Eagle Sandstone near Zimmerman Trail in west Billings, and has viewed several other fossils of exceptional quality from localities along the "Rims," but it is obvious that specimens such as these are rare.

Access to the Rims in the Billings area is difficult to impossible now because of the numerous homes and private ranchland which hug the base of the cliffs.

The Cretaceous Colorado Shale of marine origin makes up the high hills along the Yellowstone River directly south of Billings. The rock layers dip gently down to the north and east, and as a result of this a relatively complete section of the formation occurs between the town of Laurel to the west and the Eagle Sandstone cliffs to the east of Billings. Throughout the formation are found numerous limestone concretions, most of which are septarian in nature, with veins of white and brown calcite. Periodically crystals of barite and celestite are found associated with calcite crystals in small cavities within the veins themselves. Fossils, too, are sometimes found in some of the concretions, and although pelecypods predominate, some relatively nice ammonites have been found. A concretion containing some poorly preserved fossil bones (perhaps from a *Mosasaur*) was observed by the writer on one occasion. In some areas, fossils weather directly from the shale. Specimens of the ammonite *Clioscaphites* and the belemnite *Actinocamax* occur in this manner in hills adjacent to the site of the "Old South Bridge."

Most of this area consists of private land, but an area has been set aside as an "Outdoor Recreation Vehicle Site" adjacent to the Yellowstone River Bridge on South Billings Boulevard near Blue Creek. It is accessible for the purpose of collecting fossils and crystals, but be extremely alert: motorcycles and off road vehicle units make this a relatively hazardous area to stroll through. Fossils are not overly common, but when found they make a welcomed addition to any collection.

The gravels in and adjacent to the Yellowstone River south of Billings have been a source of petrified wood and occasional agates. Banded chert and red jasper also frequent the gravels, which are composed mostly of metamorphic and igneous rocks derived mainly from the mountains to the west and southwest. The petrified wood and assorted siliceous rocks often cut and polish nicely. Periods of low water, during the late summer and fall or possibly early spring, are the best times to search these gravels for potential cutting material.

Extremely well preserved fish scales and rare flattened specimens of the ammonite *Metengonoceras* can be found in the Mowry Shale. One site is located about 10.3 miles south of Billings on Hillcrest Road. The roadcut

THE BILLINGS AREA

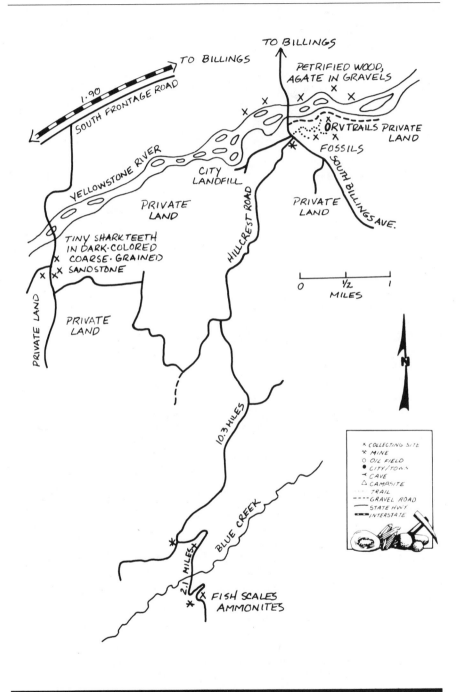

A Billings Landmark - The Rims. Outcrops of Cretaceous Eagle Sandstone form bluffs to the north and east of the city.

exposures on the Stratford Road at the southeast side of the valley are perhaps the best. The fossils are found by carefuly splitting the hard shale. Periodically, other fish remains are encountered.

A coarse-grained sandstone of Late Cretaceous age (lower Colorado Group) composed primarily of small chert pebbles, is the source of some small but well preserved shark teeth near Duck Creek. The teeth, about 1/8 inch to 1/4 inch across, occur periodically within the sandstone and can only be removed by breaking the rock around them. This is a very difficult task because quite often the shock of a hammer is sufficient to cause the teeth themselves to crumble. A number of genera and species of sharks are represented here, but their small size makes this occurrence unusual.

The sandstone layer occurs along the hillsides on private land within the lower limits of the narrow Duck Creek valley and contiguous tributary valleys. Adjacent to where Duck Creek flows into the Yellowstone River, the sandstone ledge containing the shark teeth crops out in several road cuts. These areas have been extensively collected, but as new ledges are exposed by erosion, specimens become available.

Duck Creek is located west of Billings and is best reached via the south frontage road adjacent to I-90. The King Avenue West exit on the east and the East Laurel exit on the west will provide access to the frontage road from travel on 1-90.

Access Information: Bureau of Land Management Land, private land.
Useful Maps: BLM Public Lands in Montana map: 36 *Pryor.*
U.S. Geological Survey *Billings East; Billings West, Mossmain, Mossmain SW, Soda Springs NW,* and *Yegan* Quadrangles, Montana; 7.5 Minute Series, Topographic, scale 1:24,000.

Specific References:
Gosling, A. W. and Pashley, E. F. Jr. *Water Resources of the Yellowstone River Valley, Billings to Park City, Montana.* U.S. Geological Survey Hydrologic Investigations Atlas 454, 1973.

Rice, D. D. and Shurr, G. W. *Patterns of Sedimentation and Paleogeography across the Western Interior Seaway during time of deposition of Upper Cretaceous Eagle Sandstone and equivalent rocks, Northern Great Plains.* S. E. P. M. Mesozoic Paleogeography of West Central United States, pp. 337-358, 1983.

Shelton, John W. "Trend and Genesis of Lowermost Sandstone Unit of Eagle Sandstone at Billings, Montana." *Bulletin of the American Association of Petroleum Geologists,* Vol. 46, No. 9, 1965, pp. 1385-1397.

Bluewater Creek and Red Dome east of Bridger

Several localities on private land and BLM land east of Bridger offer excellent exposures in the marine Jurassic Piper, Rierdon, and Swift formations. These rock units contain a relative abundance of the oyster *Gryphaea*, the belemnite *Pachyteuthis*, the star crinoid columnals of *Pentacrinus*, and associated fauna including several species of clams and snails, as well as ammonites. The younger Jurassic Morrison and Lower Cretaceous Cloverly formations have the polished pebbles and cobbles some interpret as gastroliths, or "gizzard stones." It is thought that perhaps as an aid to their digestive processes, certain dinosaurs swallowed and used pieces of rough gravel much in the same way that certain birds use coarse sand. The gastronomic processes may have rounded and polished the gravel in a fashion similar to a rock tumbler smoothing and polishing gemstones. The actual origin of these smoothly rounded and highly polished rocks is still debated by paleontologists. Periodically, bones of different species of dinosaurs can be found in the two formations and several relatively complete specimens of different species were

"Hey Dad, I think I found a dinosaur." A young Tom Feldman in an outcrop of the Cretaceous Cloverly Formation near the discovery of Deinonychus.

51

BLUEWATER CREEK AND RED DOME AREA

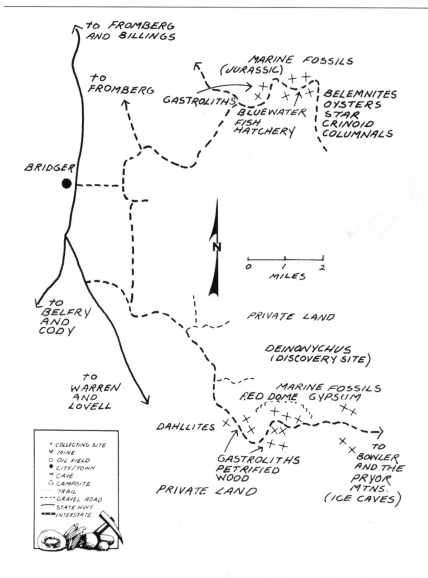

collected several decades ago (one of these finds named *Deinonychus* initiated the controversial concept of the "hot-blooded dinosaur" and is discussed in the August, 1978 issue of *National Geographic Magazine*). Along the contact of the Lower Cretaceous Cloverly Formation with the overlying Thermopolis Formation south of Red Dome, spherical concretions of the mineral dahllite occur in fair abundance. Most are broken, but they are still interesting items.

Good gravel and dirt roads provide access to both areas and fossils are generally easy to find in road cuts and nearby hills. The area is one which is tempting to explore, but respect the rights of landowners in doing so. It provides geologic study for local schools and nearby colleges. It would indeed be unfortunate if some rockhound spoiled the good relationship which presently exists between landowners and various educators.

Access Information: Private land, Bureau of Land Management land.
Useful Maps: BLM Public Lands in Montana map: 36 *Pryor.*
U.S. Geological Survey *Bluewater, Bridger,* and *Wade* Quadrangles, Montana; 7.5 Minute Series, Topographic, scale 1:24,000.
Specific References:
Ostrum, J. H. "Dinosaurs," *National Geographic Magazine,* Vol. 154, No. 2, 1978, pp. 152-185.
Richard, P.W., Ed., *Billings Geological Society 5th Annual Field Conference Guidebook,* 184 pp., 1954.

Fossils Near Pryor

Fossils in the Pryor area are extremely abundant but access to exposures may be difficult. The property here is private land and also lies within the boundaries of the Crow Indian Reservation. Check with landowners and the Bureau of Indian Affairs for details on potential collecting.

About nine to ten miles east of Pryor is a badlands region of black to dark-gray sediments of the Cretaceous Thermopolis Formation. Within these beds occur shark teeth, crocodile teeth, *pleisiosaur* bones, and pieces of turtle shell. Although remains are often well preserved, no complete specimens of any of these animals has been reported from this area.

Uranium was mined in the Pryor Mountains during the mid 1950s.

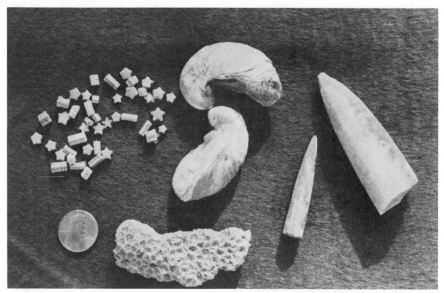

Pentacrinus *columnals, the oyster* Gryphaea, *the bullet-shaped belemnite* Pachyteuthis, *and the coral* Astrocoenia *can be collected from exposures of marine Jurassic rocks in the Pryor Mountain region.*

Twenty to twenty-two miles east of Pryor are roadcut exposures of the marine Jurassic Sundance Formation. Specimens of the belemite *Pachyteuthis* and uncommon small ammonites are found here.

While driving between these two localities one encounters numerous outcrops of the Cretaceous Cloverly Formation. It is recognized by the drab maroon and gray mudstones which predominate. This is the formation from which many remains of dinosaurs were quarried earlier in this century by eastern museums and universities.

While in the Pryor area, a visit to the Chief Plenty Coup Museum is highly recommended.

Pryor Mountains

The Pryor Mountains consist of several fault blocks which were uplifted by diastrophic processes during the Late Cretaceous and Early Tertiary periods. As a result of this mountain building and subsequent erosion, sedimentary rock layers ranging in age from Early Paleozoic to Late Cretaceous occur within and on the margins of the range. Almost all of the rock layers are fossiliferous to varying degrees, and some contain unusual mineral deposits and rocks with lapidary potential. Numerous jeep trails criss-cross the southern side of the Pryors and via these roads the entire area can be fully explored.

The Madison Limestone, a formation of Paleozoic age, reveals spirifer brachiopods, coral, and crinoid remains massed together in some outcrops. Collapsed caverns within the limestone have been the source of some secondary uranium minerals which may have originated with volcanic ash that was deposited on the Pryor Mountain region before it was exposed by erosion. The uranium minerals were discovered and prospected during the mid 1950s and several prospects were mined on a small scale, but the ore is relatively

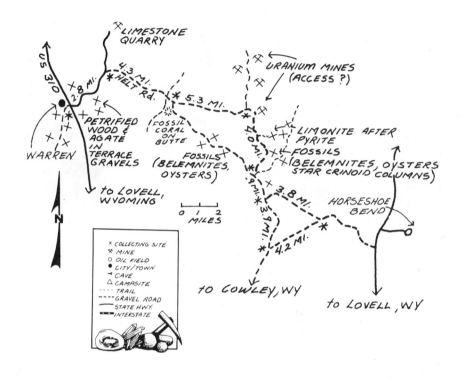

low grade and this resulted in the eventual cessation of mining. The dumps of these mines will yield nice specimens of calcite crystals, and small crystals of fluorite and pyrite, suitable for micromounts. The uranium mineral, tyuyamunite, occurs as a "powdery" coating on calcite crystals or as disseminated grains throughout the brecciated limestone. Respect any claim markers and requests by claimholders if permission is granted to visit any of the uranium mines.

In the vicinity of the uranium mines, unusually shaped nodules of banded chert are frequently found where they have weathered from outcrops of the Madison Limestone. They are often badly fractured, but at times pieces large enough to cut can be found. They are mostly gray in color, but red and brown banded varieties sometimes occur. A very fine-grained quartzite with red spots similar to pigeon-blood agate is also found, but it is not overly plentiful. Attractive cabochons have been made from both of these materials. Exposures of Late Paleozoic sediments on the flanks of the Pryors contain an abundance of limonite or geothite after pyrite pseudomorphs. These occur as clusters of

The Pryor Mountains of southcentral Montana are very scenic.

cubic crystals. Most are deeply oxidized, but some retain a very dark color with submetallic luster, and many of them, if broken, reveal the original pyrite at the center.

Along the western and southern margins of the Pryors are excellent exposures of Mesozoic rocks. The Triassic Chugwater Formation is nonfossiliferous, but its bright red color makes it quite noticeable in the landscape. Marine Jurassic formations directly overlying the Chugwater Formation, however, provide an abundance of fossils. Locally, the colonial coral *Astrocoenia* is found and the belemnite *Pachyteuthis,* oysters of the genera *Gyphaea* and *Ostrea,* and the star-shaped columnals of the crinoid *Pentacrinus,* are especially prolific. The Late Jurassic Morrison and Early Cretaceous Cloverly Formations have provided the skeletal remains of some interesting varieties of dinosaurs. This area is easily reached by relatively good gravel and dirt roads leading east from Warren, or north from Cowley and Lovell, Wyoming. If you enter the area from Warren be aware that the tops of the hills in the immediate vicinity of Warren are composed of terrace gravels of the ancestral Polecat-Shoshone River, which no longer exists as a result of stream piracy millions of years ago. A careful search of these gravels can produce some nice specimens of agatized and petrified wood, along with occasional specimens of dendritic agates.

Access Information: Bureau of Land Management land, National Forest Service land, Private land, Tribal land, and patented and unpatented mining claims.
Useful Maps: BLM Public Lands in Montana map: 36 *Pryor.*
U.S. Geological Survey *Bear Canyon, Big Ice Cave, Bowler, East Pryor Mountain, Indian Spring, Mystery Cave, Red Pryor Mountain, Wade,* and *Warren* Quadrangles, Montana; 7.5 Minutes Series, Topographic, scale 1:24,000.
Specific References:
Blackstone, D. L. "Structure and Stratigraphy of the Pryor Mountains,

Montana," *Journal of Geology,* Vol. 48, No. 6, 1940, pp. 590-618.

Gardiner, L. S., Hendricks, T. S., Hadley, H. D., and Rogers, C. P. *Stratigraphic Sections of Upper Paleozoic and Mesozoic Rocks in South Central Montana.* Montana Bureau of Mines and Geology Memoir 24, 1946.

Jarrard, L. D. *Some Occurrences of Uranium and Thorium in Montana.* Montana Bureau of Mines and Geology Miscellaneous Contribution No. 15, pp. 35-37, 1957.

Richards, P. W., Ed. *Billings Geological Society 5th Annual Field Conference Guidebook,* 184 pp., 1954.

Sahinen, U. M. *Fluorspar Deposits in Montana.* Montana Bureau of Mines and Geology Bulletin 28, pp. 34-35, 1962.

Pryor Mountains Caves

Numerous caves of various sizes and complexity can be found in the Pryor Mountains. Most of them are a solution type and have formed in the Madison Limestone of Mississippian age. So far, none have been found which contain large rooms with enormous displays of stalactites and stalagmites such as those displayed in Lewis and Clark Caverns near Three Forks or the other large caverns of the nation such as Carlsbad or Mammoth. But this is not to say that these features are not present to some degree in the Pryor Mountains caves. On a small scale, these and other more delicate features do occur. Mystery Cave, for example, is considered to be one of the better decorated caves in Montana. The entrance to Mystery Cave is located at an elevation

PRYOR MOUNTAINS CAVES

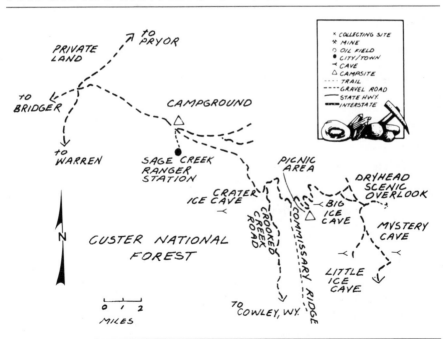

of about 7,800 feet near the crest of East Pryor Mountain. The cave displays delicate speleothems, soda straw stalactites and stalagmites, and attractive flowstone. To prevent vandalism, the entrance to Mystery Cave has been gated. Tours are not provided, but access might be gained by contacting the Bureau of Land Management Office in Billings.

One of the more frequently visited caves in the Pryor Mountains is Big Ice Cave, also located on East Pryor Mountain. Although the cave does not have much of the typical calcite deposits of other caves, the thick deposits of water ice and ice features, as the cave's name implies, are perhaps what makes it so unusual. It consists of two major rooms with a possible lower third room which is inaccessible due to the thick layer of ice on the floor of the second level. The entrance, located at an elevation of 7,530 feet on the east rim of East Pryor Mountain, also has a locked gate, but tours have been conducted by personnel of the Forest Service on weekends during the months of July and August. If interested, you may wish to contact the Custer National Forest Office in Billings for details.

Many other caves occur throughout the Pryor Mountains and many are quite challenging to the caver. It is important, however, that the unique and interesting features present in these caves be preserved, so if you plan to visit any of them, practice good cave conservation.

Access Information: National Forest Service land, Bureau of Land Management land.
Useful Maps: BLM Public Lands in Montana map: 36 *Pryor.*
U.S. Geological Survey *Big Ice Cave, East Pryor Mountain, Red Pryor Mountain,* and *Mystery Cave* Quadrangles, Montana; 7.5 Minute Series, Topographic, scale 1:24,000.
Specific References:
Campbell, N. P. *Caves of Montana.* Montana Bureau of Mines and Geology Bulletin 105, pp. 74-88, 1978.
Elliot, J. K. *Cave Occurrences in the Mississippian Madison Limestone of the Pryor Mountains, Montana.* Billings Geological Society Papers, 1963.

Big Horn Canyon

Often referred to as one of the geologic wonders of the nation, Big Horn Canyon winds its way across the north end of the Big Horn Mountains in southern Montana. Carved by the Big Horn River, its precipitous walls rise many hundreds of feet above the canyon floor. The canyon is the third deepest in North America, exceeded only by the Grand Canyon in Arizona and the Snake River Canyon in western Idaho. Recently, the canyon and adjacent area were designated a National Recreation Area by the National Park Service. Once the canyon was accessible to a daring few. Only those who were willing to float the Big Horn rapids were able to witness the wonderous sights. In 1967 the tumultuous waters of the river were slowed by the construction of Yellowtail Dam, and now a restful lake occupies the full length of the canyon. Presently a popular boating area, the canyon can be reached by anyone. Side canyons provide access to rocks of varying age in the Paleozoic rock sequence.

BIG HORN CANYON AREA

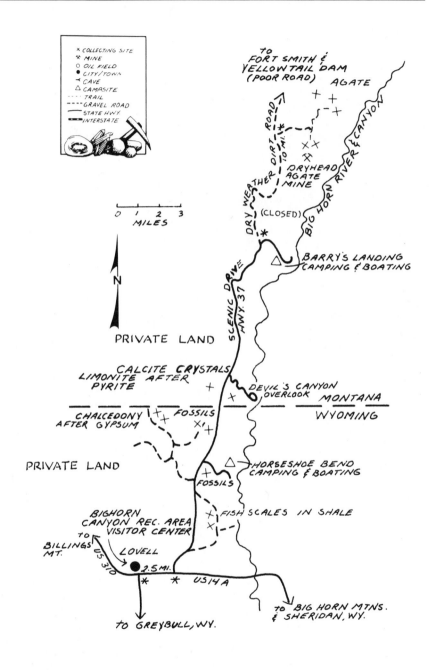

Key:
- ✗ COLLECTING SITE
- ✲ MINE
- ○ OIL FIELD
- ● CITY/TOWN
- CAVE
- △ CAMPSITE
- ···· TRAIL
- ---- GRAVEL ROAD
- —— STATE HWY
- ═══ INTERSTATE

TO FORT SMITH & YELLOWTAIL DAM (POOR ROAD)

AGATE

DRY WEATHER DIRT ROAD
10 MI.

DRYHEAD AGATE MINE

BIG HORN RIVER & CANYON

(CLOSED)

0 1 2 3 MILES

N

BARRY'S LANDING CAMPING & BOATING

SCENIC DRIVE HWY. 37

PRIVATE LAND

CALCITE CRYSTALS
LIMONITE AFTER PYRITE

DEVIL'S CANYON OVERLOOK

MONTANA

WYOMING

CHALCEDONY AFTER GYPSUM

FOSSILS

PRIVATE LAND

HORSESHOE BEND CAMPING & BOATING

FOSSILS

BIGHORN CANYON REC. AREA VISITOR CENTER

FISH SCALES IN SHALE

TO BILLINGS MT.

US 310

LOVELL

2.5 MI.

US 14 A

TO GREYBULL, WY.

TO BIG HORN MTNS. & SHERIDAN, WY.

Bighorn Canyon. The third deepest Canyon in North America.

Automobile entrance to the area from the north is limited. A paved road, State Secondary Highway 313 from Hardin, leads to the Yellowtail damsite and several marinas, but only unmaintained ranch roads, suitable for pickups and four-wheel drive vehicles, continue south from there. The best approach to the region is from the south where Wyoming Highway 37, from Lovell, will provide access to potential rock, mineral, and fossil collecting sites.

The country traversed by Highway 37 is extremely varied. Desert-like landscapes stretch for miles and the spectacular vertical walls of Big Horn Canyon can be viewed from many scenic overlooks. One of the few refuges of wild horses in North America is present in this region and it is not uncommon to see small herds of these animals feeding along the bluffs.

Although many of the rocks exposed here are highly fossiliferous, collecting fossils within the boundaries of the Recreation Area is not permitted. The Recreation Area recently came under the direction of the National Park Service and their policy is that natural features are to be enjoyed by all. The collecting of rocks, minerals, and fossils, as well as artifacts, is unlawful.

Even though rock hobby materials cannot be collected within the Recreation Area, this should not deter anyone with an interest in geology from visiting the area. It is quite remarkable and should not be overlooked by those traveling through the region. Adjacent private land has exposures of many of the same formations, and with permission, rocks, minerals, and fossils of interest might still be collected. The marine Jurassic rocks abound with the fossil oysters *Ostrea* and *Gryphaea,* the belemnite *Pachyteuthis,* and the star-shaped crinoid columnals of *Pentacrinus.* Pseudomorphs of limonite or goethite after pyrite cubes, calcite crystals and crystals of selenite are common in some outcrops of the Late Paleozoic Madison, Amsden, and Tensleep Formations. The colorful gray and maroon beds of the Lower

The Cretaceous Cloverly Formation in southcentral Montana is a source of some interesting lapidary material; jasper, chalcedony, etc.

Cretaceous Cloverly Formation west of Horseshoe Bend contain some unusual but well formed pseudomorphs of chalcendony after selenite.

Dryhead Agate

One of the most colorful lapidary materials in Montana was once found over a relatively large area south of Dryhead Creek and west of Big Horn Canyon, about thirty-five miles north of Lovell. This is the beautifully patterned fortification agate called the "Dryhead." The agates occur as nodules varying in diameter from a few inches to a little more than a foot, and each one when broken—or preferably cut—reveals a different pattern with colorful hues of red, orange, white, and lavender. Many of the nodules possess hollow centers lined with quartz crystals and secondary calcite deposits. Amethyst crystals sometimes occur. The agate nodules appear to occur most abundantly in a clay layer directly above a solid, relatively thick massive limestone layer in the Embar Formation of Late Paleozoic age. The agate's origin is somewhat of a mystery, but it is thought that the nodules formed something like concretions at the bottom of an ancient sea. The presence of this ancient sea is substantiated by the marine nature of the rocks containing the agate.

In the past, owners have allowed fee digging for Dryhead agate, but the current status of the mine is uncertain. The land is private and trespassing is prohibited. It is truly unfortunate that at least for now, this beautiful lapidary material can no longer be obtained.

For additional information, write or call:

Bureau of Land Management
Billings District
P.O. Box 2020
Billings, MT 59101

Lovell Chamber of Commerce
336 Nevada Avenue
Lovell, WY 82431

Dryhead agate - cut and polished nodule. A unique fortification agate.

Superintendent, Big Horn Canyon
National Recreation Area
P.O. Box 458
Fort Smith, MT 59035

Access Information: Private land, National Recreation Area, Bureau of Land
  Management land.
Useful Maps:
BLM Public Lands in Montana: 36 *Pryor.*
U.S. Geological Survey *Dead Indian Hill, Hillsboro,* and *Mystery Cave*
  Quadrangles, Montana; 7.5 Minute Series, Topographic, scale 1:24,000.
Specific References:
Campau, D. E., and Garrett, H. L., Eds. *Float Trip—Big Horn River from Kane,*
  Wyoming to Yellowtail Dam Site. Billings Geological Society 12th Annual
  Field Conference Guidebook, 1962.
Daggett, Jan. "Dryhead." *Lapidary Journal,* Vol. 34, No. 9, December, 1980,
  pp. 1930-1946.
Greene, W. D. "In The Beginning," *Lapidary Journal,* Vol. 26, No. 1, April,
  1972, pp. 82-90.
Prchal, Marshall, "Dryhead—Montana's Fortification Agate," *Lapidary Journal,*
  Vol. 22, No. 4, July, 1968, pp. 580-583.
Richards, P. W. *Geology of the Bighorn Canyon-Hardin Area, Montana and*
  Wyoming. U.S. Geological Survey Bulletin 1026, 1955.
Stewart, J. C. *Geology of the Dryhead-Garvin Basin, Big Horn and Carbon*
  Counties, Montana. Montana Bureau of Mines and Geology Geologic Map
  Series GM-2, 1959.
Woods, Colleen L. "Montana's Dryhead Agate," *Gems and Minerals,* No. 514,
  August, 1980, pp. 6-23.

Bearcreek Area

The year of 1889 saw the completion of the Northern Pacific Railroad to

Red Lodge, and fairly large scale production of coal from the Tertiary Fort Union Formation nearby commenced. The mining of coal was obviously related to the needs of the steam driven locomotives. Coal mining continues on a small scale today, but the steam locomotives are gone and the coal is primarily used locally for home heating.

Road cuts, mine dumps, and prospect pits in the Bearcreek and Washoe area expose sandstones and shales which can contain well preserved fossil leaf prints. Exposures on the hillsides themselves are often productive, but they are on private land. Here, as in the Fort Union deposits of eastern Montana, the leaves are those of hardwoods. Periodically, petrified logs, limbs, and stumps of trees are encountered, but not in great numbers. Rarer occurrences of fossil vertebrates (crocodile, turtle, and fish remains) have been reported.

Access Information: Private land, patented and unpatented mining claims.
Useful Maps: BLM Public Lands in Montana map: 35 *Beartooth.*
U.S. Geological Survey *Belfry* and *Red Lodge East* Quadrangles, Montana; 7.5 Minute Series, Topographic, scale 1:24,000.
Specific References:
Darrow, George. The Bear Creek Coal Field. *Billings Geological Society 5th Annual Field Conference Guidebook,* pp. 130-132, 1954.

Chromite Mines South of Red Lodge

Several unique mineral deposits occur within the highly deformed metamorphic rocks that make up the core of the Beartooth Mountains in southern Montana. Many of these deposits were mined for chromite during the 1930s and 1940s when foreign supplies were not readily available. Chromite is the major ore mineral of chromium, a metal which has many uses, the most important being that of strengthening steel.

Though not mined as extensively as the deposits within the Stillwater drainage to the north, the deposits located south of Red Lodge on Line Creek and Hellroaring Plateaus can produce samples of chromite and other interesting mineral specimens. The deposits are reached by traveling south of Red Lodge on U.S. Highway 212. This highway, or the "Cooke City Highway" as it is often called, leads to the northeast entrance to Yellowstone National Park. It traverses some of the most beautiful country in the nation, exhibiting spectacular, glaciated high mountain scenery. The sharp curves of the highway mean that the scenery should be observed from the many turnouts and scenic overlooks.

The chromite deposits can only be reached during the summer months because of snow. Even during the summer months, storms have been known to deposit significant depths of snow. It should also be mentioned that since the altitude is close to 10,000 feet, one can tire quickly from a small amount of exertion.

The Line Creek deposit is just east of the scenic overlook near the crest of the plateau. An old jeep trail near the parking area provides the easiest access. The hike in is less than one mile; motorized vehicles are not allowed.

The mine consists of both an open pit and a collapsed inclined shaft. Rocks in the area of the mine contain an assortment of minerals. The host rock, a dark green serpentine (locally called "Montana jade"), contains the chromite. The serpentine has been fashioned by some who are skilled in the art of

CHROMITE MINES SOUTH OF RED LODGE

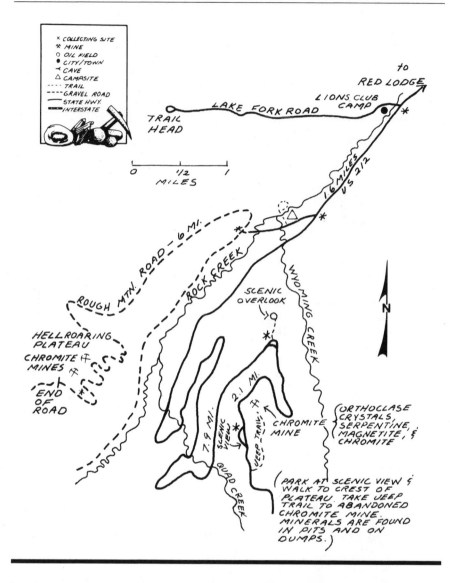

lapidary, but inclusions of other minerals prevent it from being a quality gemstone. The chromite is generally black and granular. Often weathered serpentine between the grains of chromite imparts a grey appearance to the ore. Small veins of magnetite and poorly developed chrysolite asbestos occur in some of the serpentine.

Perhaps the most interesting mineral here is orthoclase feldspar which can be found as relatively large crystals weathering from the light colored rocks in the pit. These light colored rocks are part of a small igneous intrusion, much

Collecting minerals south of Red Lodge.

younger than the Precambrian metamorphic rocks containing the chromite. The crystals are hexagonally shaped, and range in size from 1/4 inch to more than one inch in length. Most of those which are loose in the soil have been partially altered to kaolinite. Better crystals must be carefully broken from the weathered rock containing them.

Across Rock Creek Canyon from the Line Creek deposit, and at about the same elevation, are found the deposits of the Hellroaring Plateau. Similar in origin and mineralogy, but perhaps slightly more extensive, they are not as easily reached. A steep and rough mountain road must be traveled for six miles in order to reach the high mountain country where the deposit is located. It can be traveled by regular automobile, but for persons not accustomed to mountain driving, extreme caution is advised. The road is primarily maintained so that hikers can gain access to the rugged wilderness of the Beartooth Mountains, and fishermen can try their luck in the many mountain lakes which have been stocked with fish.

Access Information: National Forest Service land, patented and unpatented-mining claims.

Useful Maps: BLM Public Lands in Montana map: 35 *Beartooth.*

U.S. Geological Survey *Mount Maurice* Quadrangle, Montana; 15 Minute Series, Topographic, scale 1:62,500.

Specific References:

James, H. L. *Chromite Deposits Near Red Lodge, Carbon County Montana.* U.S. Geological Survey Bulletin 945-F, 1946.

Prchal, Marshall, "Jade Hunting in Montana," *Lapidary Journal,* Vol 23, No. 11, February 1970, pp. 1476-1478.

Rife, D. L. "Orthoclase Crystals in South-Central Montana," *Rocks and Minerals,* Vol. 40 No. 5, May, 1965, p. 329.

Schafer, P. A. *Chromite Deposits of Montana.* Montana Bureau of Mines and Geology Memoir 18, 35 p., 1937.

Zieglar, D. L., Ed. *Billings Geological Society 9th Annual Field Conference Guidebook,* 958.

Chromite Mines Near The Stillwater River

To the north of Red Lodge lies a most unique mineralized zone called the Stillwater Complex. It consists of extremely "complexed" igneous and metamorphic rocks, the most interesting being those which possess a "layered" texture. The "layering" may be the result of different minerals crystallizing at different times and settling while the rock was in a liquid or molten state. "The Complex" was mined during the 1940s for chromite, but is presently being mined for platinum and paladium. Because of exploration and development, access to the dumps of the old mines may be denied.

The Mouat and Benbow mines were the two major operations in the area and, if permission is obtained to collect from the dumps, specimens of chromite, serpentine, bronzite (a variety of enstatite), and olivine can be found in relative abundance. Other less common minerals include chrysolite, chalcopyrite, pyrrhotite, and some copper carbonates.

The Mouat Mine area near Nye is reached by paved road from either Absarokee or Red Lodge via the small community of Fishtail (Routes 307 and 419). A rough mountain road from Dean (about halfway between Fishtail and Nye on Route 419) leads to the Benbow Mine. Both of these areas are in high mountain regions and can only be reached during the summer months.

Some of the chromite was concentrated into a silvery metallic substance called "ferrochrome." Periodically, small pieces of "ferrochrome" can be found in the roadways of nearby campgrounds along the Stillwater River.

As one travels the mountain road from Dean to the Benbow Mine, a structure of concrete pillars and a crumbling foundation can be seen. Chromite was transported from the Benbow Mine high on the mountain to this structure by means of a tramway. The most impressive sight, however, is the large headframe of the tramway at the Benow site. Its size indicates the extent of mining operations here in the past.

Access Information: National Forest Service land, patented & unpatented claims.
Useful Maps: BLM Public Lands in Montana map: 35 *Beartooth.*
U.S. Geological Survey *Beehive* and *Emerald* Quadrangles, Montana; 7.5 Minute Series, Topographic, scale 1:24,000.
U.S. Geological Survey *Mt. Wood* Quadrangle, Montana; 15 Minute Series, Topographic, scale 1:62,500.

Specific References:
Czamanske, G.K. and Zientek, M.L., *The Stillwater Complex, Montana: Geology and Guide.* Montana Bureau of Mines and Geology Special Publication 92, 396 p., 1985.
Howland, A. L. *Chromite Deposits in the Central Part of the Stillwater Complex, Sweetgrass County, Montana.* U.S. Geological Survey Bulletin 1015-D, 1955.
Jones, W. R. *Igneous and Tectonic Structures of the Stillwater Complex, Montana.* U.S. Geological Survey Bulletin 107H, 1960.
Page, N. J. *Sulfide Minerals in the G and H Chromite Zones of the Stillwater Complex, Montana. U.S.* Geological Survey Professional Paper 695, 1971.

CHROMITE MINES NEAR STILLWATER RIVER

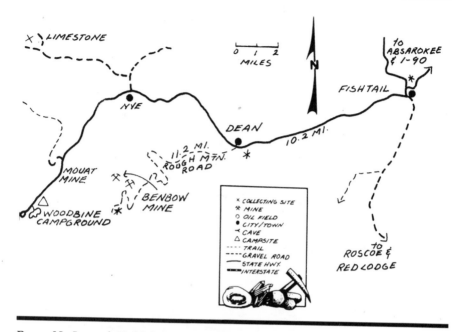

Page, N. J., and Nokleberg, W. J. *Geologic Map of the Stillwater Complex, Montana.* U.S. Geological Survey Miscellaneous Investigations Series Map I-797, 1974.

Page, N. J. *Stillwater Complex, Montana: Rock Succession, Metamorphism and Structure of the Complex and Adjacent Rocks.* U.S. Geological Survey Professional Paper 999, 1977.

Schafer, P. S. *Chromite Deposits of Montana.* Montana Bureau of Mines and Geology Memoir 18, 35 p., 1937.

Segerstrom, Kenneth, and Carolson, R. R. *Geologic Map of the Banded Upper Zone of the Stillwater Complex and Adjacent Rocks, Stillwater, Sweetgrass, and Park Counties, Montana.* U.S. Geological Survey Miscellaneous Investigations Series Map L-1383, 1982.

Cooke City—New World Mining District

High in the mountain passes north of Cooke City exists an area in which gold and silver were recovered in relatively large amounts during the early 1900s. In the vicinity of Daisy Pass, numerous mine dumps and tailings tell of a period when mining activity was much more pronounced. Because of the high elevation of 8,000 to 10,000 feet, however, mining operations were restricted to the summer season, and even then the area is free of heavy snow cover for only a few months.

Exposed here are Precambrian metamorphic rocks overlain by Lower Paleozoic sedimentary rocks and Tertiary volcanic rocks. Tertiary intrusions in the form of laccoliths, sills, and dikes occur, and the mineralization in the

COOKE CITY-NEW WORLD MINING DISTRICT

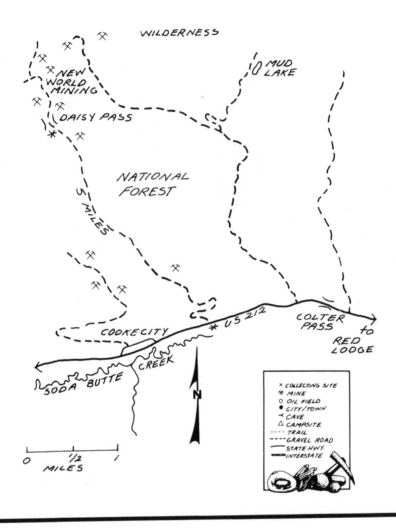

area is thought to be related to these. Dumps and tailings support considerable quantities of pyrite, most of it badly weathered. Periodically some crystals can be found. Magnetite can be found on the dumps south of Daisy Pass along with some copper minerals. The area is presently being explored for minerals indicating a possibility of renewed mining activity.

The New World Mining District is reached via several rugged mountain roads. The five-mile distance to Daisy Pass from Cooke City is barely negotiable by regular automobile. A pickup truck or a four-wheel drive vehicle is recommended for the roads in this area. Some of the most scenic country in the

The New World Mining District near Cooke City.

nation is situated here and the trails leading from Cooke City to the old mining areas offer access to those who backpack and wish to explore the Beartooth Mountains further.

The Beartooth Mountains are also noted for their unique geological features. Active glaciers of any size no longer exist here, but a few small remnants are present. Of these, Grasshopper Glacier is perhaps the most interesting. Apparently, at the time glaciers were active in these mountains, swarms of locusts became trapped in the heavy snows and were frozen. Eventually they were buried by additional snowfalls and were incorporated into the glacial mass. Many layers of these creatures can be viewed in this glacier, particularly during the later summer months when the ice is better exposed. It is a hike of considerable distance to the glacier though, since the wilderness designation of the area does not permit motorized travel. Good trails and beautiful scenery, however, make for an enjoyable outing.

Access Information: National Forest Service land, Wilderness Area, patented and unpatented mining claims.
Useful Maps: BLM Public Lands in Montana map: 35 *Beartooth.*
U.S. Geological Survey *Cooke City* Quadrangle, Montana; 15 Minute Series, Topographic, scale 1:62,500.
Specific References:
Lovering, T. S. *The New World or Cooke City Mining District, Park County, Montana.* U.S. Geological Survey Bulletin 811-A, p. 1-82, 1929.

Yellowstone National Park

The geology of the Yellowstone Park country is complex. Most of the park is underlain by relatively recent volcanic rocks with ages ranging from 60 million years to 60 thousand years (geologically young rocks). Mountain ranges

69

"Old Faithful"—A symbol of Yellowstone National Park.

consisting of folded sedimentary and metamorphic rocks border the park, and during the past few million years the entire landscape was shaped and modified by several episodes of glaciation accompanied by the continuous action of running water. The glacial features in the higher mountains, the deep canyons, and magnificent waterfalls attest to the effect of these agents of erosion. Much has been written concerning the geology of Yellowstone National Park. Several publications that present an easily read and understandable account of the park's geology are listed in the Specific Reference section for this locality.

Though located primarily in Wyoming, its proximity to Montana and its geologic significance make mention of it necessary here. Remember, however that this is a national park and the collecting of specimens is not allowed within its boundaries. This should in no way prevent rockhounds from visiting this fascinating area and viewing its unique geologic features. Written descriptions cannot do justice to its geysers, hot springs, fumeroles, and other indescribable phenomena.

In 1959, a small portion of the earth's crust northwest of Yellowstone National Park was violently disturbed by diastrophic processes. Several fault lines, displaying twenty to thirty foot displacements, a huge landslide composed of millions of cubic yards of rock, and considerable highway damage resulted from these processes.

Because of the easily visible earthquake-related features which are present here, the Forest Service established the Madison River Canyon Earthquake Area. The fairly recent geologic activity which took place here demonstrates that the mountain building processes of southwestern Montana still continue. The area is located about twenty-five miles northwest of West Yellowstone on U.S. Highway 287. A visitor center is located on top of the landslide in the mouth of the Madison Canyon, where a display of seismographs can be viewed and information concerning the earthquake is available for the interested individual.

Access Information: Federal land, National Park—NO COLLECTING!
Useful Maps: U.S. Geological Survey *Hebgen Dam* Quadrangle, Montana; 15 Minute Series, Topographic, scale 1:62,500.
U.S. Geological Survey *Yellowstone National Park, Wyoming, Montana, and Idaho*: Scale 1:125,000.
U.S. Geological Survey *Yellowstone National Park, Wyoming, Montana, Idaho*: Scale 1:1,000,000.
Specific References: Alt, David, and Hyndman, Donald, *Roadside Geology of Montana.* Missoula, Montana: Mountain Press Publishing Co., 1986, 427 pp.
Crandall, Hugh. Yellowstone—*The Story Behind the Scenery.* Las Vegas, Nevada: K. C. Publications, 1977.
Keefer, William R. *The Geologic Story of Yellowstone National Park.* U.S. Geological Survey Bulletin 1347, 1972.
Parsons, W. H. *Middle Rockies and Yellowstone.* K/H Geology Field Guide Series. Dubuque, Iowa: Kendall/Hunt Publishing Company, 1978, 233 p.
U.S. Geological Survey. *The Hebgen Lake, Montana Earthquake of August 17, 1959.* U.S. Geological Survey Professional Paper 435, 1964.
U.S. Geological Survey. *Geologic Map of Yellowstone National Park.* U.S. Geological Survey Miscellaneous Geologic Investigations Map I-711, 1972.
Yandell, M. D. *National Parkways Photographic and Comprehensive Guide to Yellowstone National Park.* Casper, Wyoming: Worldwide Research and Publishing Co., 1976.

THE GARDINER AREA

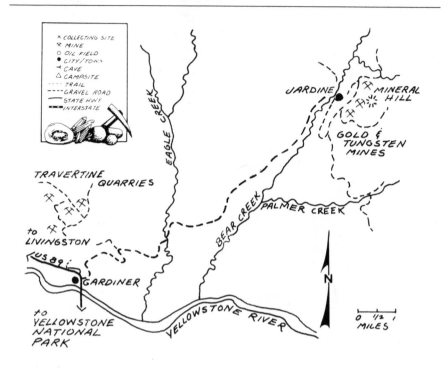

The Gardiner Area

Gardiner is perhaps most noted for being the north entrance to Yellowstone National Park. In the vicinity of Gardiner are located some interesting geological features. One of these is an extensive deposit of travertine, closely related to that being formed by hydrothermal activity at Mammoth Hot Springs south of Gardiner, just within the boundaries of the park. Travertine is the name given to the layered, vuggy limestone which owes its origin to hot spring deposition. It forms when the hot water carrying dissolved calcium carbonate reaches the surface, cools, and evaporates, thereby causing the mineral material to precipitate. Over long periods of time, thick deposits of travertine can accumulate. Several sites are presently being quarried, the material shipped north to Livingston where it is shaped into attractive blocks and pieces for buildings, patios, etc. Access to the active quarries is of course questionable, but road cuts high on the hills north of Gardiner can provide rock garden variety pieces of a less colorful travertine.

In 1866, placer gold was discovered along Bear Creek near Jardine about five miles northeast of Gardiner. Scars resulting from hydraulic mining can still be seen on the east side of the creek. It is interesting to note here that ancient stream gravels of an ancestral Bear Creek, now buried by lava flows, were also searched for gold with success. The mines at Jardine became an important source of tungsten for the nation during World War II. The tungsten is associated with gold as the mineral scheelite. The town of Jardine is still inhabited, but most of the buildings reveal their age and present the classic ghost town image.

Access Information: Private land, patented and unpatented mining claims, National Forest Service land.
Useful Maps: BLM Public Lands in Montana map: 34 *Park.*
U.S. Geological Survey *Gardiner* Quadrangle, Montana; 15 Minute Series, Topographic, scale 1:62,500.
Specific References:

Berg, R. B. *Building Stone In Montana.* Montana Bureau of Mines and Geology Bulletin 94, pp. 19-20, 1974.
Chelini, J. M. *Limestone, Dolomite and Travertine in Montana.* Montana Bureau of Mines and Geology Bulletin 44, pp. 12-13, 1965.
Fraser, G. D., Waldrop, H. A., and Hyden, H. J. *Geology of the Gardiner Area, Park County, Montana.* U.S. Geological Survey Bulletin 1277, 1969.
Seager, G. F. *Gold, Arsenic, and Tungsten Deposits of the Jardine-Crevasse Mountain District, Park County, Montana.* Montana Bureau of Mines and Geology Memoir 23, 1944.
Weissenborn, A. E. *Tungsten (in Montana).* Montana Bureau of Mines and Geology Special Publication 28, pp. 118-124, 1963.

Gallatin Petrified Forest Area

The fossil forests of Yellowstone National Park are unique in that they lie one atop another. Entire forests were buried by volcanic ash and stream-carried volcanic sediment. New forests would grow, only to be buried by the same processes. In time, the woody fibers of the trees in these buried forests were replaced by silica, thereby preserving the delicate, cellular structures of the wood.

A northern extension of these rock forests of Yellowstone can be found in southern Park and southeastern Gallatin counties. This is the area known as the Gallatin Petrified Forest, reached by traveling about fifteen miles south of Emigrant on U.S. Highway 89, and then about seven miles west on the Tom Miner Basin road to a well developed campground near the head of a beautiful mountain valley.

Wind, water, and ice have carved into the thick layers of volcanic rock in which the many petrified trees have been preserved. The logs and stumps are exposed in the cliffs and steep slopes high on the valley sides. Petrified wood can no longer be found near the campground. It was removed long ago by eager collectors. Climbing to the higher elevations and carefully searching the rocky slopes north of the campground near Ramshorn Peak will reveal pieces of petrified wood which can be collected, as well as some very large petrified logs and stumps which can be photographed. It is necessary then to hike a fair distance over rough and relatively high elevation terrain (over 5,000 feet) to reach good collecting and viewing areas, so collectors should be in good physical condition.

Much of the fossil wood's state of preservation is extremely good. Frequently, the casts of limbs and logs prove to be hollow and lined with beautiful quartz crystals, and on occasion crystals of amethyst. Some rockhounds have reported the detailed impression of leaves in the finer grained siltstones sometimes

View to the west showing ledges which contain fossil logs and wood - Tom Miner Basin.

associated with the coarser grained rock preserving the fossil wood.

Attempts have been made in the past by greedy collectors to remove large stumps and logs. When these attempts apparently failed, these majestic monoliths were destroyed with hammer and chisel. It is hoped that the established collecting limitations will discourage this kind of ignorance.

A free use permit to collect petrified wood in the Gallitin Petrified Forest is required and can be obtained at the Forest Service office in Gardiner. Since it takes several weeks to receive a permit which has to be requested by mail, it would be wise to apply for one well in advance of any trip to the area. The address of the Gardiner District Office is provided at the conclusion of this locality description.

The federal regulations concerning the amount of petrified wood that can be collected is different from that of other public land and is strictly enforced. Only a relatively small piece of petrified wood, a "souvenir," may be taken from the Gallatin National Forest. Exercising extreme selectivity in your collecting is encouraged. The size of the specimen should in no way deter one from visiting the petrified forest, however. The number of standing stumps and fallen logs of petrified wood are worth seeing. A camera can record for you the fantastic part of earth's geologic history that is preserved in the rocks at this most unique area.

Since the Gallatin Petrified Forest is in close proximity to Yellowstone National Park, and much of the area containing the petrified wood is remote, grizzly bears have frequently been sighted. The Forest Service and the Park Service publish many pamphlets regarding "Bear Country," and these should be requested when applying for a permit to collect petrified wood in the area.

NOTE: For a permit to collect petrified wood in the Gallatin Petrified Forest, send request to:

Gardiner Ranger District
Box 5, Gardiner, MT 59030   1(406)848-7375

Fossil tree stump - Tom Miner Basin.

Staurolite Crystals

Outcrops of intensely metamorphosed rocks occur northeast of the volcanic deposits preserving the fossil wood of the Gallatin Petrified Forest. The metamorphic rocks periodically contain relatively large, well formed crystals of the mineral staurolite. Staurolite frequently displays twinning with two crystals penetrating each other at either sixty or ninety degrees, thus forming a cross. Commonly referred to as "fairy crosses," these crystals occasionally occur in fair abundance throughout the rock, but are difficult if not impossible to remove.

The best areas to collect are on private land about three miles west of U.S. Highway 89 just south of Rock Creek on Crystal Cross Mountain. Here, crystals have weathered from the rock and are found loose in the soil between outcrops. Do not expect to find them in great profusion, however. Plan to spend considerable time searching for them. The area is notorious for the presence of rattlesnakes and therefore extreme caution should be exercised when looking around ledges and among clumps of grass for crystals.

Access Information: Private land, National Forest Service land.
Useful Maps: BLM Public Lands in Montana maps 33 *Madison* and 34 *Park.*
U.S. Geological Survey *Crown Butte* and *Miner* Quadrangles, Montana; 15 Minute Series, Topographic, scale 1:62,500.
Specific References:
Dorf, Erling. "Tertiary Fossil Forests of Yellowstone National Park, Wyoming." *Billings Geological Society 11th Annual Field Conference Guidebook,* pp. 253-260, 1960.
Field, L. G. "The Gallatin Petrified Forest," *Lapidary Journal,* Vol. 37, No. 8, November, 1983, pp. 1218-1223.
Prchal, Marshall. "A Petrified Forest Above the Timberline." *Lapidary Journal,* Vol. 23, No. 6, September, 1969, pp. 804-807.
Sanborn, W. B. "Fossil Forests of the Yellowstone—Part One," *Gems and Minerals,* No. 416, May, 1972, pp. 30-33.
Sanborn, W. B. "Fossil Forests of the Yellowstone—Part Two," *Gems and Minerals,* No. 417, June, 1972, pp. 24-47.

Iceland Spar Near Clyde Park

The mineral calcite, composed of calcium carbonate, is most commonly found as the sedimentary rock limestone. Frequently, it occurs in relatively large, clear single crystals, and such deposits have demonstrated potential use. Calcite which occurs in this crystalline state is commonly called Iceland Spar in reference to its initial discovery in lava flows on the island of Iceland. The cleavage rhombs of this mineral were studied and their structure evoked the early ideas concerning the atomic structure inherent in all crystalline substances.

Calcite crystals possessing optical properties were mined at several localities northeast and southeast of Livingston during the early 1940s. The cleaved portions of clear crystals, which polarize light and therefore show double refraction, were used by Polaroid Corporation in the manufacture of sighting devices for anti-aircraft weaponry. The mining ceased in the mid 1940s when the corporation developed a synthetic substitute.

The optical calcite was obtained from crystal veins occupying faults which cut sedimentary rocks of Late Cretaceous age in the region. It is thought that the calcite may have been deposited in open fissures by low temperature hot water solutions. The veins are usually a few inches to several feet wide, and sometimes trend intermittently for thousands of feet across the countryside.

The most extensively mined deposits are located on private land near Brackett Creek west of Clyde Park, a small town north of Livingston on U.S. Highway 89. Several mines were operated here, and piles of calcite litter the area. Most of the calcite on these piles is opaque but sometimes small inclusions of optical quality occur in the larger pieces. Other localities where optical grade calcite was mined are near Wilsall and south of Greycliff along Deer Creek.

An easily accessible locality for cleavable calcite can be found one mile

ICELAND SPAR NEAR CLYDE PARK

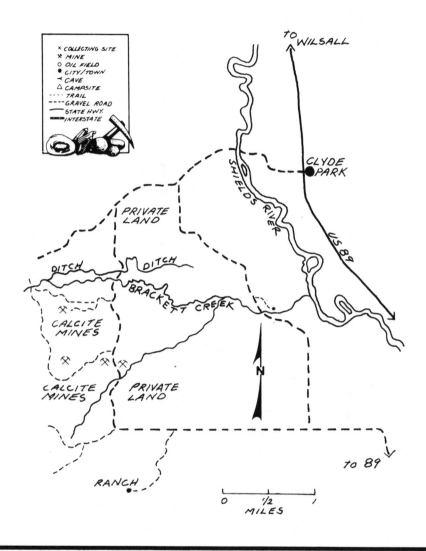

west of Hunter's Hot Springs east of Livingston and north of I-90. Here several large veins of calcite cross the road and are exposed in road cuts. The calcite is mostly opaque and diligent searching may be necessary to find transparent specimens. Several zeolite minerals, the most common being stilbite, occur with the calcite at this locality. Much of the calcite here also fluoresces a bright yellow when subjected to short-wave ultraviolet light.

Access Information: Private land.
Useful Maps: BLM Public Lands in Montana map: 34 *Park.*
U.S. Geological Survey *Chadborn, Clyde Park, Gobbler's Knob,* and *Wilsall*
Quadrangles, Montana; 7.5 Minute Series, Topographic, scale 1:24,000.
Specific References:
Stoll, W. C. *Optical Calcite Deposits in Park and Sweetgrass Counties, Montana.*
U.S. Geological Survey Bulletin 1042-M, 1958.

Karst Asbestos Deposit

There are several minerals which are commonly referred to as asbestos.
Those which have been shown to be the most useful are the amphibole and
serpentine varieties. The serpentine variety, chrysolite, often consists of thread-
like fibers which can be woven into fabric. The amphibole variety is brittle
and has generally been used in building insulation products. Several deposits
of these minerals have been located in Montana, but few of them have been
large enough to be economically productive. One of the deposits which has
been mined to some degree is the Karst Deposit located about thirty miles
southwest of Bozeman along the Gallatin River.

The type of asbestos mineral mined from the Karst Deposit was of the
amphibole variety and was found occurring as dike-like bodies in highly
contorted metamorphic rocks. It is recognized by its fibrous texture and light
color.

Although the deposit was discovered as early as 1900, it was not until 1935
that larger scale mining operations took place. Several open cuts were made
to expose the asbestos which was mined, shipped, and processed to be used
as an insulating material for buildings.

The mine lies high on a mountain slope about .75 mile west of the Karst
Guest Ranch located about twenty-two miles south of Gallatin Gateway on
U.S. Highway 191. A poor road and trail provide access to the mine and if
permission to visit the mine is obtained, it might be advisable to walk rather
than drive.

Access Information: National Forest Service land, patented mining claim.
Useful Maps: BLM Public Lands in Montana map: 33 *Madison.*
U.S. Geological Survey *Garnet Mtn.* Quadrangle, Montana; 15 Minute Series,
Topographic, scale 1:62,500.
Specific References:
Perry, E. S. *Talc, Graphite, Vermiculite,* and *Asbestos in Montana.* Montana
Bureau of Mines and Geology Memoir 27, pp. 36-39, 1948.

The Bozeman Area

Bozeman Pass

Several zeolite minerals as well as calcite can be found in exposures of the
Livingston Formation in the vicinity of Bozeman Pass about ten miles east
of Bozeman. Since it is unlawful to park anywhere along interstate highways
except in an emergency, it would be best to gain access to the frontage road
near the pass.

Small calcite crystals, heulandite, and some laumontite crystals are present
in the rocks exposed here. Searching should be confined to railroad and
highway cuts to the east of Bozeman Pass. The minerals are not especially
abundant but by breaking some rock, a serious collector should be rewarded

with specimens that may be suitable for micromount and possibly thumbnail collections.

Hyalite Canyon

Southeast of Bozeman is scenic Hyalite Canyon. The canyon derives its name from the rare presence of hyalite opal in rocks on Hyalite Peak at the head of the canyon. The opal is transparent to transluscent and occurs as botryoidal coatings on some of the rock exposed in the area. Considerable searching and breaking of rock may be required to obtain specimens. Reaching the locality requires a somewhat strenuous hike of approximately seven miles from the end of the road. For those amibtious enough to attempt, the scenery alone is worth the effort.

Corundum Deposits

Three deposits of corundum occur on predominately private land in the mountainous terrain west of Gallatin Gateway. One deposit was briefly operated during the early 1900s, and all three were extensively explored during the mid-1940s as potential sources of abrasive corundum. They were found to be relatively minor deposits and could only be worked at high cost.

The corundum is not of gem quality and is found as fairly large blue-gray, barrel-shaped crystals scattered throughout lenses of what appears to be metamorphic rock. The origin of the corundum here has been disputed since most corundum elsewhere in Montana has been associated with igneous instrusions.

Minerals near Norris

Several miles east of Norris on State Highway 84, a number of mine tailings can be seen on both sides of the road. The major minerals found in this area consist of pyrite, quartz, some galena and sphalerite, and rarely, a feldspar mineral which shows a colorful chatoyancy on cleavage planes. The writer is not aware of any being utilized for lapidary purposes but suspects the possibility if pieces large enough can be obtained.

About six miles west and south of Norris is Revenue Flats, named after the Revenue Mine. The road to this location is a little rough, but when dry can be traversed easily by four-wheel drive vehicles. There are numerous open shafts of unknown depth scattered throughout the area.

Access Information: Private land.
Useful Maps: BLM Public Lands in Montana map: 33 *Madison*.
U.S. Geological Survey *Anceney* and *Bozeman* Quadrangles, Montana; 15 Minute Series, Topographic, scale 1:62,500.
U.S. Geological Survey *Norris* and *Maltbys Mound* Quadrangles, Montana; 7.5 Minute Series, Topographic, scale 1:24,000.
Specific References:

Clabaugh, S. E. *Corundum Deposits of Gallatin and Madison Counties Montana.* U.S. Geological Survey Bulletin 696-B, 1950.
Clabaugh, S. E. *Corundum Deposits of Montana* U.S. Geological Survey Bulletin 983, p. 67-77, 1952.

THREE FORKS AREA

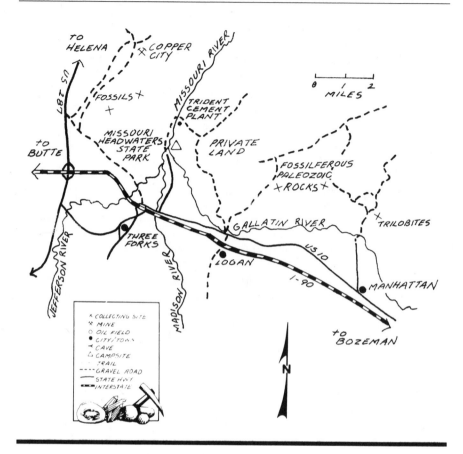

Three Forks Area

The community of Three Forks received its name because it is adjacent to the confluence of three streams which make up the Missouri River. In fact, an area designated The Missouri River Headwaters State Monument has been established just north of the town. Located here are scenic campsites for those who may be traveling with RV camping units and wish to spend some time in this most interesting region.

Rocks varying in age from Precambrian to recent outcrop here, and classic localities for fossils and geologic features can be found. As in some other areas of the state, the unique geological features exposed here provide an outdoor classroom for the geology departments of many local as well as out-of-state colleges and universities. Montana State University is located about thirty miles to the east, and Indiana University operates a summer geologic field station in the northern Tobacco Root Mountains south of Cardwell to the west. With regard to most of the areas mentioned here, the land is privately owned. A good relationship exists between the landowners and the educators who use these areas to train potential geologists. Be certain to obtain permission before visiting any of these areas so that this relationship is not jeopardized.

Fossils near Three Forks

Fossils of Early and Late Paleozoic age are relatively common in rock outcrops in the general vicinity of Three Forks. Tributaries of the Gallatin, Madison, and Jefferson rivers have carved into the predominantly folded Paleozoic rocks producing limestone ridges and shale valleys. Certain layers of these rocks will yield, with careful searching, numerous varieties of invertebrate fossils.

By digging into exposures of the Cambrian limestones and shales located about four miles north of Manhattan along Nixon Gulch, fairly well preserved trilobites of the genus *Bathyuriscus* can be found. Most often, they occur as fragments, but occasionally, a relatively complete specimen can be obtained. The specimens are found by splitting the shale layers with a chisel or a sharp knife. When first uncovered, the shale is quite moist and should be allowed to dry before any preparation work is attempted. Good specimens are somewhat reminiscent of the fine trilobite genus *Elrathia* that is found in central Utah, except the preservation is perhaps not quite as good. Frequently, small dark circular cap-like brachiopods occur with the trilobite debris in many of the beds.

Nearby, exposures of the Devonian Three Forks Shale often produce some well preserved brachiopods of the spirifer type. Corals and crinoid columnals are also found, but good exposures of this formation are not common. Fossils are most easily found in gullies where the formation is exposed by running water.

The Mississippian Madison Limestone is generally a good source of fossils, but they are normally contained within the limestone, and are difficult if not impossible to remove. Outcrops of these Paleozoic rocks also occur near Sappington and again near Lewis and Clark Caverns. Here, too, the rocks contain fossils.

In some areas of the Gallatin Valley extremely attractive opalized wood has been located. The geologic age of this wood is not known, and its source has not been visited by the writer. Most of it apparently occurs on private land and access is doubtful.

During the Middle Tertiary Period, sediments were deposited in lake basins occupying the intermontane valleys of this region. The bones of many types of animals were buried and preserved in these sediments and have received considerable attention by many paleontologists. Outcrops of these sediments occur to the east and south of Three Forks. Similar deposits have been studied in the vicinity of Pipestone, just west of Whitehall.

Sappington Mica Mine

One of the few deposits actually mined for mica in Montana is located south and east of Sappington Junction west of Three Forks. The deposit is located on private land and was worked for a short period of time in the 1940s. The mica is primarily muscovite and occurs in several pegmatite bodies exposed in the area. The size of individual sheets of mica found here was relatively small compared to the very large sheets that have been obtained from

LEWIS AND CLARK CAVERN STATE PARK

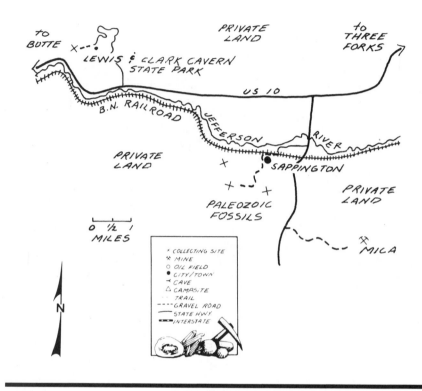

pegmatites in the Black Hills region of South Dakota. The cores of the pegmatites near Sappington consist mainly of white quartz, but some zones of rose quartz have been reported. The pegmatites containing the mica here are cutting metamorphic rocks, mainly schists and gneisses of Precambrian age.

Lewis and Clark Cavern State Park

Lewis and Clark Cavern State Park is not one of the more well known cavern areas in the nation, but it equals many of them in spectacular beauty. The caverns contain an abundance of unique features such as stalactites, stalagmites, columns, and minor features like speleothems, helictites, and clusterites.

Though actually discovered in 1892, the caverns were not exploited until the early 1900s. They are presently a state park, and guided tours are provided.

The caverns occur in the massive Madison Limestone of Mississippian age. It is thought that the caverns themselves began to form about 65 million years ago during the Late Cretaceous Period when the Rocky Mountains were forming. The diastrophic action in the region at that time may have initiated the erosional processes in the limestone, and as the older rocks were exposed, ground water dissolved and deposited limestone to produce the cavern features.

Because of the interesting deposits of calcium carbonate in the shape of mythological and fairy tale personalities, the caverns are popular with tourists, and large numbers of them visit the park each year. Among these are many rockhounds, who, because of their knowledge of and appreciation for geologic processes, perhaps view them differently than do most tourists.

The state park can be reached by driving twenty-two miles west of Three Forks, or ten miles east of Cardwell on old U.S. Highway 10. The caverns are open daily from May 1st to September 30th. Hours of operation are from 8:00 a.m. to 6:00 p.m., and an admission fee is charged.

Access Information: Bureau of Land Management land, private land, state land.
Useful Maps: BLM Public Lands in Montana map: 33 *Madison.*
U. S. Geological Survey *Jefferson Island, Manhattan,* and *Three Forks* Quadrangles, Montana; 15 Minute Series, Topographic, scale 1:62,500.
Specific References:
Campbell, N. P. *Caves of Montana,* Montana Bureau of Mines and Geology Bulletin 105, pp. 108-111, 1978.
Heinrich, E. W *Pegmatite Mineral Deposits in Montana.* Montana Bureau of Mines and Geology Memoir 28, pp. 23-25, 1948.
Perry, E.S. *Morrison Cave, Lewis and Clark Cavern State Park.* Butte, Montana: T. Greenfield, Inc., 1946.
Perry, E. S. *Highlights of Geology Between Three Forks and Whitehall.* Billings Geological Society 1st Annual Field Conference Guidebook, pp. 56-59, 1950.
Robinson, G. D. *Geology of the Three Forks Quadrangle, Montana.* U.S. Geological Survey Professional Paper 370, 1963.

The Townsend Area

The Townsend Valley between Three Forks and Helena supports a variety of geological features, many of which may be of interest to the rock hobbyist.

Several areas along the east flank of the Elkhorn Mountains were mined intermittently from 1866 up to a few decades ago. The discovery of placer gold near Radersburg began a period of exploration in the region and eventually lode deposits containing gold, silver, lead, and zinc were found and mined. Many mine dumps and tailings to the west of U.S. Highway 287 between Toston and Winston are potential sources of some unique minerals.

Near Radersburg, an interesting deposit of titaniferous magnetite has been determined to be a beach concentration of Late Cretaceous age. The titanium iron ore, located on private land, has been mined and shipped to the Trident Cement Plant near Three Forks where it was used as a flux.

Nearby, an outcrop of the Cambrian Meagher Limestone, also on private land, has been quarried because of the unusual patterns in the rock. Referred to as "Black and Gold Marble," the rock is quite interesting. It was apparently quarried for use as a dimension stone but no considerable quantity of material has been removed from the small quarry, productive for only a short period of time.

The Jo Dandy Mine and the Ruby Mine, west of Radersburg, have yielded some interesting minerals, but the mines are patented claims and permission must be obtained before visiting them. At the Jo Dandy Mine, to the north, small crystals of wulfenite have been found. Quartz, calcite, galena, errusite, and hemimorphite are also present.

At the Ruby Mine to the south, smithsonite and hemimorphite are found.

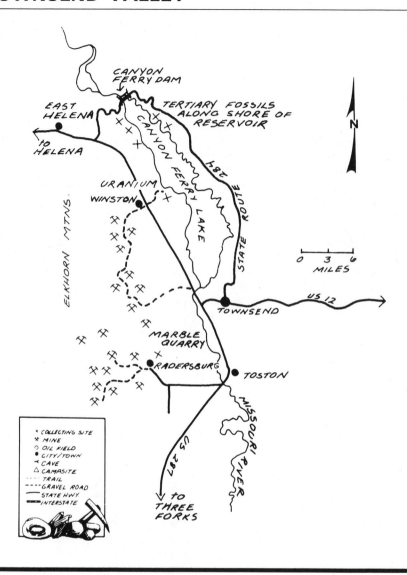

Some very small crystals of vanadinite have been reported.

A uranium mineral identified as metatorbernite has been found in carbonaceous rocks east of Winston. The uranium was deposited from overlying Oligocene sediments of volcanic origin. There has been no major mining since a single attempt to strip mine the deposit showed that it could not be mined economically. Private land must be crossed to reach the deposit, and the uranium mineral, which occurs as yellowish-green micaceous flakes, is difficult to see in ordinary light. Searching for it would be easiest at night,

NEIHART MINING DISTRICT

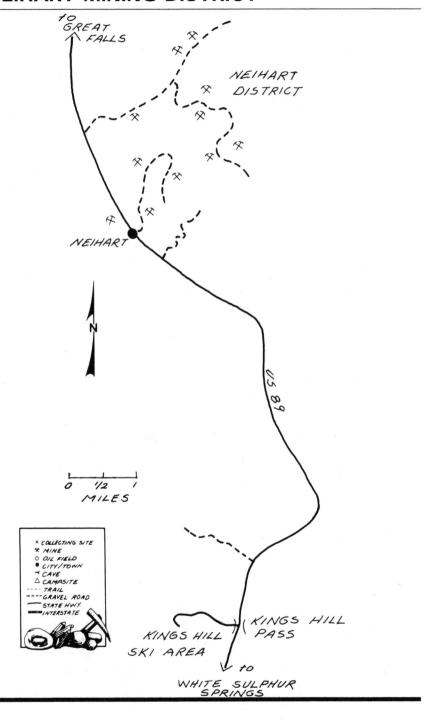

since it fluoresces a bright yellow-green under short-wave ultraviolet light.

Mid Tertiary sedimentary rocks, not unlike those exposed in the areas near Three Forks and Pipestone, occur along the northern shores of Canyon Ferry Reservoir north of Townsend. These deposits have been the source of many species of fossil mammals. Specimens continue to be exposed by the wave action along the shore, but this same action tends to destroy them in the process. Periodically, specimens of bone, teeth, and other skeletal structures are discovered by boaters and fisherman. The collecting of such fossils is presently not allowed on public land, but perhaps can be undertaken on private land with permission of the owner. Rockhounds are nonetheless reminded of their obligations with respect to the collection of rare and unusual fossils on any type of land.

Fairly colorful agate, jasper, petrified wood, and common opal also occur along the shore of the reservoir. Some of the material has been reported to have lapidary potential.

Pyrite, quartz, azurite, and malachite (some of cutting quality) can be found at the Argo Mine. The mine site is reached by driving on Highway 284 on the east side of the Canyon Ferry Reservoir to Hellgate Gulch and then up the canyon for several miles. The road is relatively good but has frequent curves. Because the road winds, it would perhaps be wise to stop while viewing the magnificent scenery in the canyon. The Argo Mine was operated in the early part of this century with gold being the mineral of primary importance.

To the north and east of Townsend near White Sulphur Springs lie the mining districts of Castle and Neihart. Both were important producers of various minerals in their heyday but for the most part now lie idle. Castle is presently a ghost town, but Neihart, which is situated along U.S. Highway 89 between White Sulphur Springs and Great Falls, sustains a small population. Kings Hill, a major ski area nearby, provides the old mining community with business during the winter months, but the hustle and bustle that took place here decades ago when the mines were active is gone.

Discovered in 1881, the deposits near Neihart have produced close to 17 million dollars worth of minerals. Though silver was the chief metal being sought here, lead, copper, gold, and zinc were also found. The veins and other ore bodies containing the minerals of these metals occur primarily in Precambrian metamorphic and sedimentary rocks along with younger igneous intrusions.

The Castle Mining District lies southeast of White Sulphur Springs and can be reached by traveling about seventeen miles south of White Sulphur Springs on U.S. Highway 89, about twelve miles east on state highway 294, and then north ten miles on a gravel and dirt road near Lennep. It is out of the way of major transportation routes, and has therefore experienced a fate much different from that of Neihart. When the minerals became too expensive to mine, the town was for the most part abandoned, and now, because of disuse, few of the original structures in the district remain.

Prospecting in the district began in 1881, but it wasn't until several years later that actual mining began. A considerable amount of production has taken place since that time with silver, lead, zinc, copper, and manganese being the contributing metals. The ore deposits are of several types including fissure veins, replacement mineralization, and contact mineralization between Paleozoic limestones and igneous rocks. It has been determined by

CASTLE MOUNTAINS MINING DISTRICT

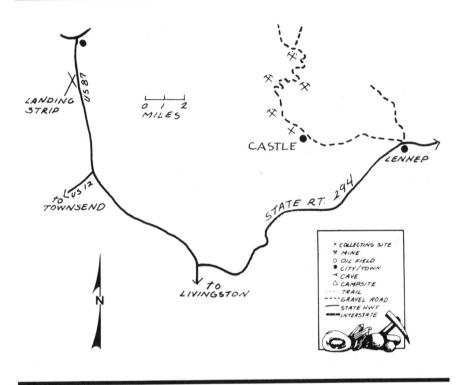

geologists that the mineralization took place as several episodes, each responsible for the deposition of certain primary elements.

If access can be gained to the dumps and tailings in this district, they may produce specimens of pyrite, sphalerite, galena, chalcopyrite, cerussite, quartz, and some carbonates and oxides of copper, iron, and managanese.

Access Information: Private land, patented and unpatented mining claims.
Useful Maps: BLM Public Lands in Montana map: 24 *Castles.*
U.S. Geological Survey *Castle Town* Quadrangle, Montana; 7.5 Minute Series, Topographic, scale 1:24,000.
U.S. Geological Survey *Neihart, Devil's Fence,* and *Radersburg* Quadrangles, Montana; 15 Minute Series, Topographic, scale 1:62,500.
U.S. Forest Service Visitors Map; Lewis and Clark National Forest (Jefferson Division) Montana.
Specific References:
Aalseth, E. P. and Lorenz, H. W. "Third Day Road Log—Helena to Townsend." *Billings Geological Society 10th Anniversary Field Conference Guidebook,* p. 178-182, 1959.
Becraft, G. E. *Uranium in Carbonaceous Rocks in the Townsend and Helena Valleys, Montana.* U.S. Geological Survey Bulletin 1046-G, 1958.

Berg, R. B. *Building Stone in Montana.* Montana Bureau of Mines and Geology Bulletin 94, p. 18, 1974.

DeMunck, V. C. *Iron Deposits in Montana.* Montana Bureau of Mines and Geology Information Circular 13, pp. 39-40, 1956.

Freeman, V. L. *Geology of Part of the Townsend Valley, Broadwater and Jefferson Counties, Montana.* U.S. Geological Survey Bulletin 1042-N, 1958.

Klepper, M. R. *Geology and Mineral Deposits, East Flank of the Elkhorn Mountains, Broadwater County, Montana.* U.S. Geological Survey Professional Paper 665, 1971.

Mertie, J. B., Jr., Fischer, R. P., and Hobbs, S. W. *Geology of the Canyon Ferry Quadrangle, Montana. U.S. Geological Survey Bulletin 972, 1951.*

Pardee, J. T. *Geology and Ground Water Resources of Townsend Valley, Montana.* U.S. Geological Survey Water Supply Paper 539, 1925.

Schafer, P. A. *Geology and Ore Deposits of the Neihart Mining District, Cascade County, Montana.* Montana Bureau of Mines and Geology Memoir 13, 1935.

Schell, E. M. *Ore Deposits of the Northern Part of the Park (Indian Creek) District, Broadwater County, Montana.* Montana Bureau of Mines and Geology Bulletin 36, 1963.

Winters, A. S. *Geology and Ore Deposits of the Castle Mountain Mining District, Meagher County, Montana.* Montana Bureau of Mines and Geology Bulletin 54, 1968.

General Helena Area

In 1864, placer gold made Last Chance Gulch, now a main street of Helena, one of the most famous places in Montana. By 1910, the gravels of the gulch had yielded approximately 16 million dollars in gold.

Several rumors concerning the gulch and its remaining riches have endured over the years. One of these tells of small gold nuggets appearing from a water faucet, presumably since the area's water supply originated at the head of Last Chance Gulch. Another story evolved around the gravels which were excavated for building foundations along the gulch. It was said that enough gold could be panned from these gravels to pay for the construction of the buildings. These stories are of course far fetched, but so was the real wealth produced from Last Chance Gulch and the surrounding territory.

The gold in the gravels of the gulch originated in the lode deposits which occurred along Last Chance Creek and its tributaries. It was sought using a variety of methods from simple panning to large scale dredging. The larger dredges were operated from 1935 to 1945, when they were shut down for economic reasons.

To the north and west, similar operations near Rimini, Austin, Marysville, Wilborn, and Lincoln have produced, since the late 1800's, quantities of gold valued in the millions. These are interesting places to visit and the stream gravels may yet produce gold for the prospector. Lode deposits in these areas were also developed and the mine dumps may yield minerals of interest to the collector. Most common, of course, is pyrite, but other sulfides, carbonates, and oxides have been reported. Because of their age, these mine dumps and tailings, like so many others in Montana, have undergone considerable weathering, and mineral specimens of fair size may be very difficult to find. Diligent investigating may uncover specimens of micromount or thumbnail collection quality.

Gold placer deposits also occur along both sides of the Missouri River north and east of Helena, but unlike the placers discussed earlier, these often contain commercial quantities of abrasive and gem quality corundum (sapphires). The State Historical Society Museum in Helena near the State Capitol Building displays some of the early mining equipment and ores found at nearby mining camps. The exhibit represents a part of Montana's heritage, and is well worth a visit.

Access Information: Private land, patented and unpatented mining claims.
  Useful Maps: BLM Public Lands in Montana maps: 22 *Avon* and 23 *Townsend.*
U.S. Geological Survey *Helena* Quadrangle, Montana; 15 Minute Series, Topographic, scale 1:62,500.
Specific References:
Boulter, G. W. *Placer Deposits of Last Chance Gulch, Helena, Montana.* Billings Geological Society 1st Annual Field Conference Guidebook, pp. 72-73, 1950.
Knopf, Adolph. *Ore Deposits of the Helena Mining Region, Montana.* U.S. Geological Survey Bulletin 527, 1913.
Pardee, J. T., and Schrader, F. C. *Metalliferous Deposits of the Greater Helena Mining Region, Montana.* U.S. Geological Survey Bulletin, 842, 1933.
Sahinen, U. M. "Metalliferous Deposits in the Helena Area, Montana." *Billings Geological Society 10th Anniversary Field Conference Guidebook,* p. 129-140, 1959.

Helena Area Sapphire Mines

In 1865, sapphires were first discoverd in Montana in the terrace gravel deposits along the Missouri River northeast of Helena. At the time, these deposits were being worked for placer gold and the sapphires were a byproduct that clogged the riffles in sluice boxes and dredges. When their value was recognized, mining the sapphires became almost as important as mining gold. In fact, several companies were organized specifically for the purpose of mining sapphires, but fluctuating prices and the general instability of the market caused them to change hands or cease operations. The development of synthetic corundum virtually eliminated the need for natural corundum as a source of abrasives and commercial mining today is primarily restricted to gem quality stones.

Igneous dikes containing sapphires have been located along the river upstream from the terrace gravel deposits containing sapphires. Since these terrace gravels were deposited by the Missouri River, it is quite possible that the sapphires contained in them originated from dikes located in the area, and were carried by the river along with the other material making up the terrace deposits.

All of the operating sapphire mines in the Helena area are located in terrace gravel deposits and the sapphires found at each locality are similar. Although some of the operations allow fee digging and rent equipment, it is suggested that you bring your own. It should include good shovels, picks, assorted mesh screens (preferably 1/2-inch mesh and 1/8-inch mesh), a whisk broom (for sweeping small gravel from cracks in the bedrock where sapphires may have been trapped), tweezers, and of course small containers in which to place any sapphires that you may find. The operators are usually very willing to provide screening and searching instructions to those who have never before hunted sapphires. Some of the mines have equipment that will wash and sort your screened gravel for you, thus simplifying the work necessary to retrieve

HELENA AREA SAPPHIRE MINES

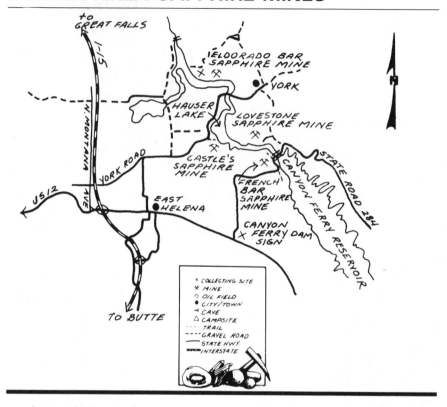

sapphires which may be present. Be sure to check with the owners of the mines to see what services they offer. Rules, services, and fees can change from year to year. The operating status of these mines can very quickly change with ownership so it may be wise to check in Helena before driving out.

Eldorado Bar Sapphire Mine

The Eldorado Bar Mine is located about ten miles downstream from Canyon Ferry Dam on the east shore of Hauser Lake. Fee digging for sapphires is allowed from May 1st through October 1st. Hours of operation are generally 7:00 a.m. to 6:00 p.m. Some equipment, such as shakers, shovels, and picks, is available for rent. Screened gravel can be washed by hand, or, for a small fee, processed by an electric jig. Camping facilities, some with electrical hookups, are available at a nominal cost, and a limited supply of grocery items, as well as a faceting service, is provided at the gem shop near the electric jigs.

For further information, write or call:

Eldorado Mine
6240 Nelson Road
Helena, MT 59601
(406) 442-7960

Howard Feldman digging gravel in search of sapphires in the Helena area.

Spokane Bar Sapphire Mine

The Spokane Bar Mine is situated on a high gravel terrace about five miles downstream from Canyon Ferry Dam and west of Hauser Lake. Public fee digging for sapphires is permitted with some equipment available for rent. Digging is confined to virgin or previously unprocessed ground which will enhance one's chances of finding sapphires. Buckets of pre-screened gravel may be purchased if one chooses not to dig. Customers have the choice of washing their screened gravel themselves near the edge of the reservoir, or for a small fee, taking advantage of the work-saving motorized jigs. For those interested in large quantities of sapphires, full-day concentrate "runs" are available. For the customers who find gem quality sapphires, services such as faceting and heat treatment are offered at the fully equipped rock shop on the premises. Bags of potential sapphire-bearing gravel are also available for purchase. These will be shipped, via mail, worldwide. Dry camping with a few lakeshore sites are provided at no cost to customers. The mine is open to the public all year and hours of operation are from 9:00 a.m. to 5:00 p.m., seven days a week.

Shoreline activity at Eldorado Bar Sapphire Mine.

For more information, write or call:

Russell Thompson
4363 Hart Drive
Helena, MT 59601
(406) 227-8989

Lovestone Sapphire Mine

The Lovestone Sapphire Mine is located on the east side of the Missouri River a few miles downstream from Canyon Ferry Dam. The mine caters mainly to those interested in relatively large quantities of sapphires but does sell bags of concentrate at $60 per bag.

The mine's primary operation centers around a concentrate half-day "run" which consists of about fifty cubic yards of gravel. This is washed and produces about ten buckets of concentrate. The cost of the run is $500 and at the time of this writing was yielding 250 to 1,000 carats of sapphires per run.

Customers may camp at the mine site but it is recommended that camping units be self-contained or that customers camp at public campgrounds near Canyon Ferry Dam.

The mine is open from May 15th through November 15th with hours of operation from 8:00 a.m. to 8:00 p.m. daily.

For further information, write or call:

Lovestone Mining Company
4440 Jimtown Road
Helena, MT 59601
(406) 475-3714

Access Information: Private land, patented and unpatented mining claims.
Useful Maps: BLM Public Lands in Montana map: 23 *Townsend.*
U.S. Geological Survey *Hauser Lake, Lake Helena,* and *Nelson* Quadrangles, Montana; 7.5 Minute Series, Topographic, scale 1:24,000.
U.S. Geological Survey *East Helena* Quadrangle, Montana; 15 Minute Series, Topographic, scale 1:62,500.
Specific References:
Birdsall, Mura. "Eldorado Sapphires," *Lapidary Journal,* Vol. 33, No. 2, May, 1979, pp. 524-536.
Broughton, P. L. "In Search of Sapphire," *Rock and Gem,* Vol. 2, No. 5, June, 1972, pp. 22-25.
Clabaugh, S. E. *Corundum Deposits in Montana,* U.S. Geological Survey Bulletin 983, pp. 34-44, 1952.
Knoblach, Earl, and Knoblach, Beverly. "Hunting Sapphires in Montana," *Lapidary Journal,* Vol. 21, No. 9, December, 1967, pp. 1180-1181.
Munday, V. F. "Sapphire Mining in the Big Sky Country," *Lapidary Journal,* Vol. 31, No. 10, January, 1978, pp. 2190-2193.
Young, Marjorie. "Sapphires on Eldorado Bar," *Gems and Minerals,* No. 383, August, 1969, pp. 28-31.

Jefferson City Area

Numerous mines and gold placer deposits occur in the general vicinity of Jefferson City. The placer deposits were worked as early as 1865, but proved to be inferior to those at Helena or Alder Gulch near Virginia City. They were soon abandoned, but lode mining in the district continued for some time after that. From 1902 until 1957 nearly 4 million dollars in gold and silver was obtained from placer operations in Jefferson County, most of it from placers near Jefferson City.

The majority of mineralization is associated with the intrusion of the Boulder Batholith. The batholith itself is granite-like, but the minerals were found in deposits which were connected with contact metamorphism of preexisting rocks surrounding the batholith. There is also some evidence which relates some of the mineralization to a later period of igneous activity.

There are primary and secondary uranium minerals in the southern part of this area, near the towns of Boulder and Basin. Their occurrence has spawned several "health" mines where people are invited, for a fee, to bask in the radiation present in the mines. The positive effects of such actions have been debated, however.

Those who may want to try hobby panning the gravels of streams in the Jefferson City area for gold should be aware that cassiterite, the major source of tin, has been found here in the nodular form known as "wood tin." It apparently is found as small rounded masses, and because of its density, it will settle to the bottom of the pan during the panning procedure.

Several years ago when the writer last visited this area the old gold dredge on Prickly Pear Creek, twelve miles north of Boulder, was still present. The tailings left by this behemoth as it made its way upstream in search of gold are only partially overgrown by vegetation, and are evidence of man's disregard for the beauty of nature when riches are at stake. It is true that this was perhaps the most economic way of recovering the gold contained in the gravels of the stream, but perhaps more than economics

JEFFERSON CITY AREA

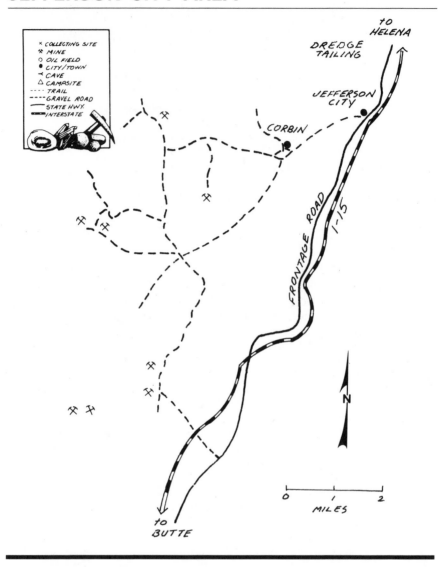

should be considered when ventures such as this are undertaken.

Barite near Basin
Although there are numerous gold mines in the general vicinity of Basin, some of the more interesting collecting can be done on private land around Indian Head Rock two miles west of Basin. Here one can find golden barite crystals. They are relatively common in an area north of the interstate highway, but thus far no gem quality specimens have been found. On the south side of the river, crystals can be found in the cliffs and the talus below them. This

Gold Dredge which used to exist on Prickly Pear Creek north of Boulder. Typical of those used throughout the state.

area requires crossing the river and is more difficult to reach.

Access Information: Private land, patented and unpatented mining claims.
Useful Maps: BLM Public Lands in Montana maps: 22 *Avon* and 23 *Townsend.*
U.S. Geological Survey *Jefferson City* Quadrangle, Montana; 15 Minute Series,
   Topographic, scale 1:62,500.
Specific References:
Becraft, G. E., Pinckney, D. M., and Rosenblum, Sam. *Geology and Mineral Deposits of the Jefferson City Quadrangle, Jefferson and Lewis and Clark Counties, Montana.* U.S. Geological Survey Professional Paper 428, 1963.
Demunck, V.C. and Ackerman, W.C. *Barite Deposits in Montana.* Montana Bureau of Mines and Geology Information Circular 22, pp. 18-20, 1958.
Roberts, W. A., and Gude, A. J., III. *Uranium Deposits West of Clancy, Jefferson City, Montana.* U.S. Geological Survey Bulletin 998-F, 1953.
Roby, R. N., Ackerman, W. C., Fulkerson, F. B., and Crowley, F. A. *Mines and Mineral Deposits (Except Fuels), Jefferson County, Montana.* Montana Bureau of Mines and Geology Bulletin 16, 1960.

South of Great Falls

Several mines are located west of Rogers Pass near Lincoln. Most of them were operated for lead and copper. At the Mike Horse Mine the minerals pyrite, chalcopyrite, galena, quartz, cerussite, and sphalerite are found. Some copper carbonate minerals have also been reported along with rare amethyst in small vugs of the host rock.

In roadcuts along the interstate highway and frontage roads between Craig and Hardy, the zeolite minerals stilbite, laumontite, and mesolite, as well as calcite and rare amethyst can be collected. Remember, however, it is illegal to park along an interstate highway except in cases of emergency.

Great Falls Area

Continental glaciation during the Pleistocene epoch was quite extensive in northern Montana, and consequently, the landscape around Great Falls is subdued. Rocks of Early to Late Cretaceous age occur in the region, but exposures are confined primarily to deep gullies and bluffs along the Missouri River and various tributary streams.

Marine shales and sandstones of the Late Cretaceous Colorado Group appear to predominate to the north and west of Great Falls, and prized fossil specimens from these rocks have been reported, especially along the drainage basins of the Sun, Teton, and Marias rivers.

The Missouri River Breaks

Some extremely scenic and rugged country can be found along the Missouri River downstream from Fort Benton. Most of this region is very primitive and much of it can be reached only by boat. The area around the White Cliffs is particularly spectacular, and the area as a whole can provide some unique rockhound experiences. A mixture of different land designations prevails here, with sections of state-owned, federal, BLM, and private lands, and a good map is essential to ensure that various laws and regulations are not inadvertently violated.

A region of diverse and relatively accessible rock formations occurs to the east and southeast of Big Sandy. Here, too, the land designations are varied and local inquiry may be necessary to prevent accidental trespass. The rocks exposed in the Birch Creek and Sand Creek areas near the Choteau and Blaine County boundary have produced marine fossils, many of them from the Late Cretaceous Bearpaw Shale. The area lies to the south of the Bearpaw Mountains, and numerous faults make the geology complex.

State Route 236, which leads southeast from Big Sandy, is a relatively well maintained road that eventually crosses the Missouri River north of Winifred. It provides general access to regions of good rock hobby potential. It is a large area and fossils include both marine and non-marine types. Most side roads in the region are poorly maintained and should definitely be avoided during rainy weather. The rock units which appear here are the Late Cretaceous Claggett Shale, Bearpaw Shale, and Judith River Formation.

The region near the confluence of the Judith River and the Missouri River is noted for the spectacular dinosaur finds of Charles Sternberg and Edward Cope during the late 1800's. Discoveries of dinosaurs continue to be made in the Judith River Formation here, but it must be remembered that fossils of this sort are indeed rare and are of extreme scientific importance.

Tempskya Wood

Lower Cretaceous and Late Jurassic rocks exposed in areas to the west and southwest of Great Falls have also yielded some very interesting fossils. Of these, fossil wood appears to be the most common. An unusual fossil wood that is periodically found in the Early Cretaceous rock exposures belongs to the genus *Tempskya*. *Tempskya* specimens are highly prized by collectors because of their relative rarity and unusual structure. Transverse sections of *Tempskya* "logs" reveal irregularly shaped circular features, often called "eyes" by collectors. These apparently represent cross-sections of stems which grew parallel to the roots of the plant to form the "false trunk" of this unusual fossil.

Lapidary artists have attempted to capitalize on the unique structure of the wood, but most specimens when cut reveal a pitch black interior. It has been discovered that by soaking a cut slab of the *Tempskya* wood in bleach for some time, the "eye" pattern of the stems and roots are exposed. Cabochons have been fashioned from the bleached material with varying degrees of success. Typical examples of *Tempskya* wood are on display at the Earth Science Museum in Loma.

Most of the scientific research which has been conducted with regard to the genus *Tempskya* seems to indicate it is restricted to Lower Cretaceous rocks, but some finds in the Great Falls area may suggest occurrences in late Jurassic rocks as well. Whether or not these finds actually prove that the relative age of *Tempskya* needs to be extended, is still being debated. Some investigators feel that the specimens found in Late Jurassic rock outcrops may have actually been derived from Lower Cretaceous rocks exposed nearby, and just transported by fairly recent gradational processes.

Several localities between the small communities of Manchester and Vaughn west of Great Falls have been sources of *Tempskya* wood. Most of the exposures from which the wood has been reported are located on private land north of old U.S. Highway 89 and are recognized by their white color.

Other areas where *Tempskya* wood has been collected are located west of Ulm near Square Butte and eight to ten miles east of Cacade. Farther east of Cascade, the Hound Creek area has produced some good specimens, and it is in this region where the controversial Jurassic aged specimens discussed earlier were found. Rattlesnakes are common where *Tempskya* wood is found, so it would be advisable to watch where one walks and reaches.

Baby Dinosaurs and Fossil Eggs Near Choteau

The recent discovery of some very small dinosaur bones in rocks of Late Cretaceous age near Choteau has led to an extremely fascinating study. The presence of what appears to be a large nesting site of *Hadrosaur* dinosaurs has prompted paleontologists from the Museum of the Rockies in Bozeman to make an annual trek to this region to seek additional data. Not only have the bones of juvenile and adult dinosaurs been recovered, but several clutches of fossil eggs have been retrieved from the fine-grained sediments exposed here. As a result, one site has been affectionately named "Egg Mountain."

The fact that fossilized remains of juvenile dinosaurs occur in nests indicates that adult dinosaurs cared for their young. This is a characteristic quite unlike that of typical cold blooded animals and is therefore supporting evidence for the current warm blooded dinosaur concept being investigated by many paleontologists today. This information perhaps inspired the paleontologists to assign the name *Maiasaura peeblesorum* to this new genus and species of dinosaur. The name *Maiasaura* is based on the latin word referring to "maternal lizard" (because of the assumed relationship between the adult and offspring). The species designation was made to honor the persons upon whose land the discovery site is located.

The well articulated skeletons of so many juveniles generally rules out death by predation, or the bones would more than likely have been scattered. It has been suggested that the deaths and the preservation of the animals here were probably due to some cataclysmic event. A flood, mud flow, or perhaps heavy ash fall from a nearby volcanic eruption may have provided the scientists with such a rare and relatively complete find.

GREAT FALLS AREA

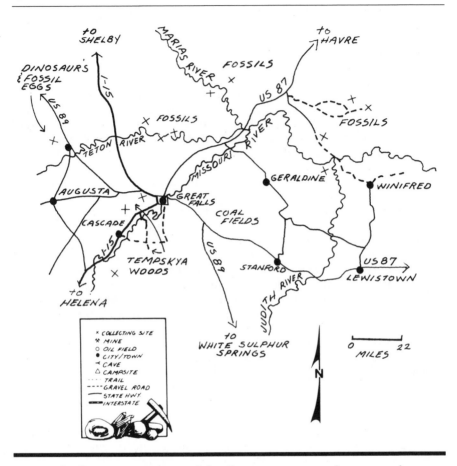

Juvenile dinosaur remains and fossil eggs are extremely rare, and, consequently, this is probably one of the more important paleontological discoveries in the world. It is definitely one which should be left to the professionals to examine. Many unanswered questions regarding the life habits and the extinction of dinosaurs may be resolved on the basis of discoveries made here.

The various rock clubs of Montana decided that this unique find should be recognized in another way. They recommended that *Maiasaura peeblesorum* be made the state fossil. On February 22, 1985, this dinosaur officially became Montana's state fossil.

There is currenty a paleontology program offered that allows interested persons an opportunity to spend time in the Egg Mountain area and assist with the professional digging and research being conducted there. For more information, write to the Museum of the Rockies in Bozeman.

Access Information: Private land, BLM land, state land, and federal land.
Useful Maps: BLM Maps: *Belt, Fort Benton, Great Falls North,* and *Great Falls South. Scale 1:100,000.*

ROCHESTER MINING DISTRICT AND CRYSTAL BUTTE

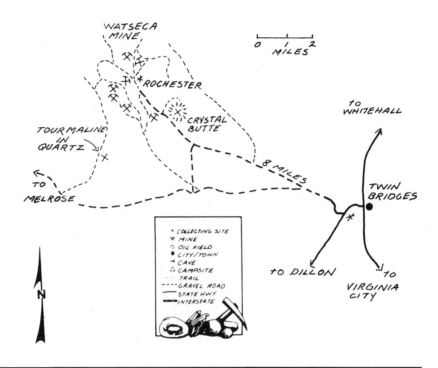

U.S. Geological Survey *Choteau, Havre,* and *Lewistown Maps; Scale 1:250,000.*
Specific References:
Horner, J. R. "The Nesting Behavior of Dinosaurs," *Scientific American,* April
    1984, pp. 130-137.
Tidwell, W. D. *Common Fossil Plants of Western North American.* Provo, Utah:
    Brigham Young University Press, 1975, pp. 125-126.
Zeller, R. A., Jr. *North American Species of Tempskya and Their Stratigraphic
    Significance.* U.S. Geological Survey Professional Paper 874, 1976.

Rochester Mining District and Crystal Butte

The Rochester District lies about eleven miles northwest of Twin Bridges
and can be reached by a good gravel and dirt road. The Highland Mountains
on the north and the McCarthy Mountains to the south provide an interesting
setting. Since it does not occur at a high elevation and the climate is obviously
arid, the water necessary for large scale placer operations is not present and
most of the mining here has been of lode deposits. The ore deposits occur
primarily as veins in metamorphic rock, as contact deposits along the margins
of Paleozoic limestones and igneous instrusions, or as replacement deposits

in limestone. The age of the vein deposits has been determined to be Early Tertiary, probably Eocene or Oligocene. The contact deposits are more than likely associated with the Late Cretaceous or very Early Tertiary intrusions present in the area.

The mineral deposits of the Rochester District were exploited mainly for gold and silver. Mining began on a small scale during the late 1800s when placer operations were attempted but proved to be too difficult to work because of the lack of water. The early exploration was quickly followed by underground mining and during the productive years the district produced a fair quantity of high grade ore. During the writer's last visit to the area, the Watseca Mine was showing signs of activity.

The dumps and tailings, although deeply weathered, should, with careful searching, produce specimens of pyrite, galena, sphalerite, malachite, azurite, chrysocolla, arsenopyrite, quartz, and very rare specimens of cerussite, vanadinite, pyromorphite, and anglesite. Be particularly observant for open shafts among the tailings as they may be both partially collapsed and partially hidden from view.

Crystal Butte is a large mass of mainly white quartz which apparently contains numerous vugs or cavities. These cavities in the rock contained nicely terminated crystals of quartz and many years of weathering had allowed crystals to accumulate on the slopes of the butte. It was because of the occurrence of these crystals that the butte received its name. Crystals no longer occur abundantly on the butte, but specimens might be found with diligent searching. When the writer visited the area, several claim markers were posted about the butte, and a large amount of quartz had been removed from its crest. Apparently this feature represents a source of high-purity quartz and even though maps show the butte to be located on BLM land it would be wise to check the claim status before attempting to collect crystals.

Crystal Butte is reached by a faint jeep trail which leaves the main road about eight miles west of Twin Bridges. The trail is next to a grove of trees and leads up the gully to the north. A one-mile drive along the trail will take one to Crystal Butte, which can be recognized by its white color. A vehicle with good clearance is recommended, but the distance can be walked if necessary.

Access Information: BLM land, patented and unpatented mining claims, private land.
Useful Maps: BLM Public Lands in Montana map: 32 *Dillon.*
U.S. Geological Survey *Twin Bridges* Quadrangle, Montana 15 Minute Series, Topographic, scale 1:62,500.
Specific References:
Chelini, J. M. *Some High-Purity Quartz Deposits in Montana.* Montana Bureau of Mines and Geology Bulletin 54, pp. 21-22, 1966.
Lawson, D. C. *Directory of Montana Mining Enterprises for 1980.* Montana Bureau of Mines and Geology Bulletin 115, pp. 31-37, 1981.
Sahinen, U. M. *Geology and Ore Deposits of the Rochester and Adjacent Mining Districts, Madison County, Montana.* Montana Bureau of Mines and Geology Memoir 19, 1939.

The Virginia City Area

Following the discovery of rich placer deposits of gold at Bannack, prospectors spread out to locate others. This quickly led to the discovery of placer gold in Alder Gulch and the eventual establishment of Virginia City as the second territorial capital of Montana.

The immense tailings between Virginia City and Alder are mute testimony to the intense search for gold in this area. Huge dredges chewed into the stream gravels, spit out the unwanted rock and kept the gold within. Gold still lies hidden beneath the rugged terrain, but even with the present gold price, costs keep the number of operating mines to a minimum.

Virginia City is now a popular tourist attraction during the summer months. Many of the original buildings have been restored. Numerous curio and gift shops provide souvenirs and occasionally some offer lessons in the art of panning gold.

Northwest of Virginia City, on the southern edge of the Tobacco Root Mountains, lie several small mining districts. The Tidal Wave district east of Twin Bridges is typical. Placer operations initiated the search for gold and later some lode deposits of gold, silver, and lead were investigated. The ores occur in

TIDAL WAVE MINING DISTRICT

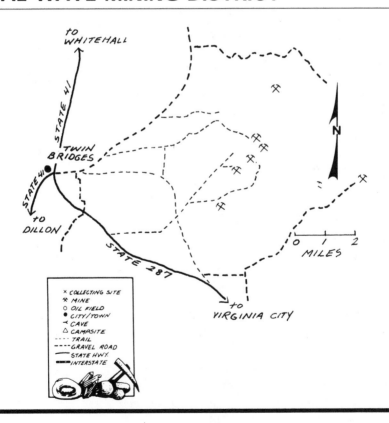

Virginia City is a popular tourist attraction in southwestern Montana.

both Precambrian metamorphic and Paleozoic sedimentary rocks. The mine dumps and tailings may produce some of the various sulfide minerals associated with deposits of this nature.

Northeast of Sheridan near Indian Creek, at a relatively high elevation, a deposit of calcium carbonate (cave onyx) has been developed. The calcite is mostly white in color, but light brown and honey-colored banded masses are commonly found. The deposits were apparently formed by the movement of groundwater near the contact of Paleozoic sedimentary rocks. The source of the calcite may have been the solution of adjacent carbonate rocks. The deposit has been quarried for material to be used for Terrazzo, exposed aggregate panels, and stone chips for landscaping. Carvings similar to the popular Mexican onyx have also been made from this material.

Volcanic rocks exposed in road cuts along State Highway 287 between Virginia City and Ennis contain vugs and cavities lined with zeolite and carbonate minerals. Adjacent to them are dark colored, banded metamorphic rocks containing red almandine garnet. The metamorphic rocks are frequently cut by pegmatite dikes which contain white, glassy, and sometimes rose colored quartz, as well as fine cleavable masses of pink microcline feldspar. The view toward the east here is also very spectacular, revealing the rugged glaciated peaks of the Madison Range.

In the steep road cut just past Ruby Dam south of Alder, metamorphic rocks containing calcite, siderite, opalite, and some graphite occur. The rock in parts is actually a marble, and, in some elongated cavities, tiny crystals of calcite and siderite can be found. Associated with these carbonates are veinlike occurrences of white to pink and brown opalite. No gem quality opal was observed at this locality, however. The graphite occurs as very small flakes and grains in the gray schist outcrops near the southeast end of the road cut. It is not very common here and may be considered just an oddity for collectors. The graphite obviously does not occur in the same magnitude as it does southeast

MINERALS NEAR VIRGINIA CITY

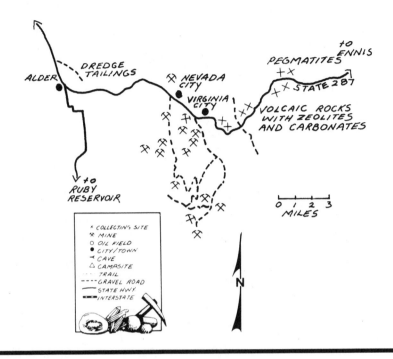

of Dillon where it was mined on a small scale. The Dillon graphite deposits were discovered in 1899 and initially thought to be lead. Between 1902 and 1944, graphite was mined sporadically on a more or less profitable basis. In 1944, the mines were closed because foreign supplies could be obtained more economically.

Perhaps the most impressive mineral in this area is garnet, which abounds in some of the dark metamorphic rocks common to the region. The road cuts below Ruby Dam exhibit some typical rocks containing a high percentage of garnet associated with the black mineral hornblende.

Gem quality almandine garnets, suitable for faceting, are frequently found by screening the terrace and stream deposits in the valleys of the Ruby River and Sweetwater Creek. An ideal place to search for them is along the shores of the Ruby Reservoir above Ruby Dam. The garnets vary in size, although most are very small. A series of screen meshes would best separate the gravel from the fine sand, and the small gravel can be washed in the reservoir. The distinctive deep red color of the garnets serves to distinguish them from the other rock particles. Obviously, not all the garnets found will be of gem quality, but time and patience should reward a collector with good specimens. The best time to search for garnets along the shores of the reservoir is during periods of low water. Early spring, before the streams begin carrying meltwater from the mountains, or during the late fall when the streams are running very low, would be ideal times. At no time, however, should one dig in the road cuts along the east shore of the reservoir. The Highway Department has placed warning signs, and a fine could result if the warning is disobeyed.

About fifteen miles south of the Ruby Dam along the Sweetwater Creek road to Dillon there is a very interesting deposit of volcanic rock. It is an attractive rock with bands of varying widths. Shades of yellow, brown, and red make up the colors of the bands. Technically described as silicified interbedded tuff, and difficult to obtain in large pieces, this material is suitable for decorative book ends and similar products. The rock does not take a high polish and therefore does not fashion well into cabochons although some of good quality have been seen. The rock was quarried as a source of Terrazzo, but apparently the operation was abandoned after a short period of time. The quarry containing the rock, referred to as "Montana onyx," is located on private land and inquiry concerning access should be made before attempting to collect here.

Access Information: Private land, patented and unpatented mining claims, BLM land.

Useful Maps: BLM Public Lands in Montana maps: 32 *Dillon* and 33 *Madison*.

U.S. Geological Survey *Alder, Belmont Park Ranch, Copper Mtn., Metzel Ranch, Ruby Dam,* and *Sheridan* Quadrangles, Montana; 7.5 Minute Series, Topographic, scale 1:24,000.

U.S. Geological Survey *Twin Bridges, Virginia City,* and *Waterloo* Quadrangles, Montana; 15 Minute Series, Topographic, scale 1:62,500.

Specific References:

Balster, C. A. *Geology of the Southern Tobacco Root Mountains, Madison County, Montana.* Montana Geological Society 18th Annual Field Conference Guidebook, pp. 89-92, 1967.

Balster, C. A., Groff, S. L., and Johns, W. M. *Third Day Geologic Road Log, Virginia City to Branham Lakes via Sheridan.* Montana Geologic Society 18th Annual Field Conference Guidebook, pp. xv-xx, 1967.

Berg, R. B. *Building Stone in Montana.* Montana Bureau of Mines and Geology Bulletin 94, pp. 19 and 26, 1974.

Bragg, Addison, R. "Vigilante Country." *Billings Geological Society 11th Annual Field Conference Guidebook,* pp. 15-19, 1960.

Johns, W. M. *Geology and Ore Deposits of the Southern Tidal Wave Mining District, Madison County, Montana.* Montana Bureau of Mines and Geology Bulletin 24, 1961.

Tansley, W., Schafer, P. A., and Hart, L. N. *A Geological Reconnaissance of the Tobacco Root Mountains, Madison County, Montana.* Montana Bureau of Mines and Geology Memoir 9, 1933.

RUBY RESERVOIR AREA SOUTH OF ALDER

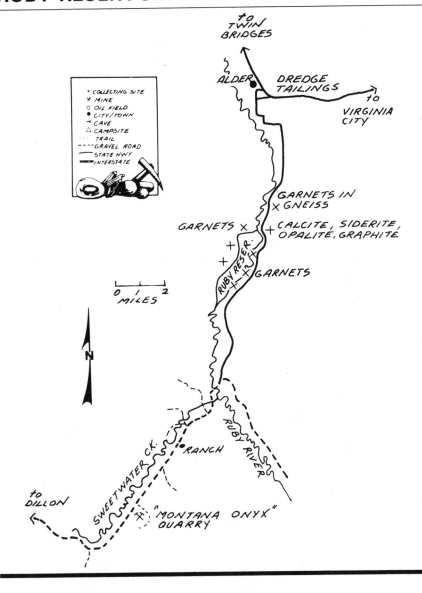

Talc Deposits Near Dillon and Ennis

The source of talcum powder is the mineral talc, a hydrous silicate of magnesium. It is very soft and easily scratched by the thumbnail. It possesses a "soapy" feel and is often called "soapstone."

Even though there are many deposits of talc throughout Montana, two major areas have been exploited on a relatively large scale. One area lies southeast of Dillon, and the other southwest of Ennis. The talc at both these facilities occurs in dolomitic marbles of Precambrian age, and are thought to have formed when hydrothermal solutions passed through the rocks and altered them before they were uplifted and exposed by erosion. Masses of sillimanite and kyanite also occur in rock outcrops near the talc deposits along with schists and gneisses containing garnet and staurolite.

The talc operations at Johnny Gulch near Ennis have produced a very fine beige colored dendritic talc, which when carved is very attractive. Whether or not this material is still available from the mine is not known, but specimens may possibly be purchased from local rock dealers.

The talc deposits have been worked for many years and operations in both areas continue at the present. Access to the mines and nearby areas is questionable because of the hazards associated with the mining operations and the fact that the land adjacent to the mines is privately owned. Care should be taken not to trespass.

Access Information: Private land, patented and unpatented mining claims.
Useful Maps: BLM Public Lands in Montana maps: 32 *Dillon* and 33 *Madison*.
U.S. Geological Survey *Cameron* and *Varney* Quadrangles, Montana; 15 Minute
  Series, Topographic, scale 1:62,500.
Specific References:
Berg, R. B. *Talc and Chlorite Deposits in Montana*. Montana Bureau of Mines
  and Geology Memoir 45, 1979.
Heinrich, E. W. *Sillimanite Minerals South of Ennis, Madison County, Montana*.
  Montana Bureau of Mines and Geology Miscellaneous Contribution 10,
  1948.
Heinrich, E. W. *Sillimanite Deposits of the Dillon Region, Montana*. Montana
  Bureau of Mines and Geology Memoir 30, 1950.
Perry, E. S. *Talc, Graphite, Vermiculite, and Asbestos in Montana*. Montana
  Bureau of Mines and Geology Memoir 27, 1948.

Bannack and Argenta

One of the first major discoveries of gold in the state occurred in 1862 when the yellow metal was found in the gravels of Grasshopper Creek southwest of what is now Dillon. A small community began to arise here, and in 1864 Bannack became Montana's first territorial capital. The rocks outcropping in the immediate vicinity of Bannack are limestones of Late Paleozoic age. Since the early prospectors noted that the gravels upstream from Bannack failed to yield any significant amounts of gold, the source of the gold had to be in the limestones nearby. It was soon discovered that the lode deposits were associated with igneous rocks which had intruded the limestones.

Even though the lode deposits were subsequently exploited, the construction of several ditches was undertaken to provide the water necessary to sluice the gravels of Grasshopper Creek for the gold that they contained. The remains of these ditches can be seen high on the mountainside to the south of Bannack.

During the years of 1895 and 1896, a series of large electric-powered gold dredges were launched in Grasshopper Creek and considerable quantities of gold were recovered. Lode mining also continued in the district and although production was intermittent up to the mid 1900s the total amount of placer and lode production is estimated to be about 12 million dollars. Bannack is presently being restored and has been established as a state park. Many of

BANNACK-ARGENTA AREA

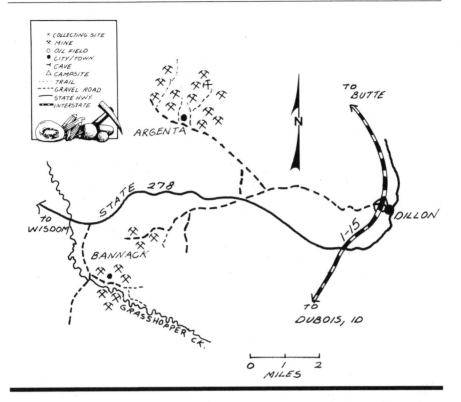

the original buildings still stand and markers have been placed in areas where important structures once stood. The area is well worth a visit since it is so rich in history with stories revolving around villainous road agents and the infamous Henry Plummer. The state park designation makes the area a fairly popular one, and therefore success in collecting from mine dumps and tailings is uncertain.

Bannack can be reached by traveling west of Dillon on State Highway 278 for about fifteen miles and then five more miles south on a well-marked dirt and gravel road. Be sure to watch for the Bannack State Park sign along the highway.

Mining did not begin in the Argenta area until the Bannack area had been fully explored. Unlike the Bannack region, however, silver and lead were the more important metals produced from the Argenta District. Also, very little placer activity took place, so the vast majority of the production came from lode deposits.

The first ore smelter in the state was constructed at Argenta in 1865 and was used to treat ore which was mined strictly in the Argenta District, but after the construction of several other smelters in the same area, ore from other districts was also accepted.

Bannack - Montana's First Territorial Capital.

The uniquely ornamented smokestack is all that remains of the smelter at Glendale where ores from the Hecla Mining District were processed.

The type of rock exposed in the Argenta area is similar to that exposed at Bannack. It is sedimentary, but in general much older. Most of the ore bodies occur in these rocks where mineral-bearing solutions were apparently injected either into fissures or along bedding planes, but some contact metamorphism deposits do exist within the district.

At the time the writer visited the district, several mines showed signs of activity, so be certain inquiries are made before collecting mineral specimens here. Much of the ore mined has been extremely oxidized, but certain sulfides as well as various copper carbonates occur on the dumps and tailings of the old mines.

To reach Argenta, drive ten miles west of Dillon on State Highway 278 and then north on a good gravel road for about five miles.

Access Information: State land, patented and unpatented mining claims, private land.

Useful Maps: BLM Public Lands in Montana maps: 31 *Big Hole* and 32 *Dillon.* U.S. Geological Survey *Argenta* and *Bannack* Quadrangles, Montana; 7.5 Minute Series, Topographic, scale 1:24,000.

Specific References:

Alt, Dave. "Bannack-Gravels of Gold Are Gone But Not The Gold Rush Dream." *Montana Magazine,* September/October, 1982, pp. 34-36.

Bragg, A. R. *Vigilante Country.* Billings Geological Society 11th Annual Field Conference Guidebook, pp. 15-19, 1960.

Geach, R. D. *Mines and Mineral Deposits* (Except Fuels), *Beaverhead County, Montana.* Montana Bureau of Mines and Geology Bulletin 85, pp. 41-66 and 78-85, 1972.

Shenon, P. J. *Geology and Ore Deposits of Bannack and Argenta, Montana.* Montana Bureau of Mines and Geology Bulletin 6, 1931.

The Hecla District

About fifteen miles west of Melrose is perhaps the greatest mineral producing area in Beaverhead County. The Hecla District is located in high mountain country where glaciation has produced some very spectacular scenery.

Most of the minerals mined here were those containing silver and lead, but zinc, copper, and gold were also present. The ore bodies occur, for the most part, in lower Paleozoic rocks and were possibly formed when solutions containing the minerals rose from magma which intruded the region sometime after the Paleozoic Era.

Rich ore deposits were discovered in 1872 and the first shipments took place the following year. By 1965 the total production of the Hecla District was valued at a little more than 19.5 million dollars. As with most productive mining districts, a series of predictable events followed the discovery of the rich ores. Trapper City and Lion City arose as a result of the operations, and then in 1875, a relatively large smelter was constructed down the valley at Glendale to accomodate the ores from the mines in the Hecla and other nearby mining districts.

Very little of these small but bustling mining communities remains. Rotting timbers and crumbling foundations are all that exist of Trapper City and Lion City today. Glendale is also a ghost town but the smoke stack of the old smelter stands, a testimonial to the considerable efforts which took place here during the previous century.

HECLA MINING DISTRICT

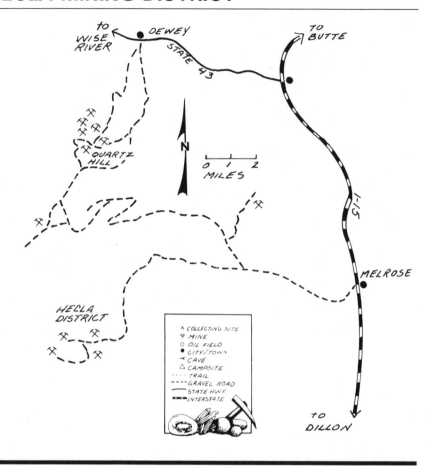

Access Information: Private land, National Forest Service land, patented and unpatented mining claims.

Useful Maps: BLM Public Lands in Montana map: 32 *Dillon.*

U.S. Geological Survey *Earls Gulch* and *Melrose* Quadrangles, Montana; 7.5 Minute Series, Topographic, scale 1:24,000.

U.S. Geological Survey *Vipond Park* Quadrangle, Montana; 15 Minute Series, Topographic, scale 1:62,500.

Specific References:

Geach, R. D. *Mines and Mineral Deposits (Except Fuels), Beaverhead County, Montana.* Montana Bureau of Mines and Geology Bulletin 85, pp. 111-120, 1972.

Karlstrom, T. N. V. *Geology and Ore Deposits of the Hecla Mining District, Beaverhead County, Montana.* Montana Bureau of Mines and Geology Memoir 25, 1948.

Crystal Park

A most unique collecting site occurs about twenty-six miles south of Wise River in the Pioneer Mountains. Peaceful meadows, beautiful forests, and majestic peaks provide an ideal setting for Crystal Park, where rockhounds may dig quartz crystals.

The many pits occurring on the slopes, suggest that this locality is popular with rockhounds. The area is extensive, and as the sign posted at the parking lot indicates, crystals of amethyst and of clear and smoky quartz can be found with conscientious effort. Good crystals do not come easily, though. They are found only by digging into the hillside, and this means work.

The serious collector should plan to bring shovel, pick, and some assorted mesh screens to sift the dirt and loose rock. Extremely nice crystals have been taken from this locality, but quality comes with time and patience. Just a few hours spent here will more than likely result in disappointment, but a day or two may result in finding something worthwhile.

Several nearby campgrounds offer adequate facilities for those who wish to remain for a spell and enjoy some very beautiful scenery, as well as a "good dig." Crystal Park itself has picnic tables and well maintained restroom facilities.

The Wise River country is scenic, and the Wise River road provides access not only to Crystal Park but to some of the more beautiful country in western Montana. The road changes from typical washboard to a nice paved highway as one enters the national forest land about 4.5 miles south of Wise River. The paved road winds through the valley of the Wise River with its numerous campsites and summer homes for about 11.2 miles before becoming a narrow dirt and gravel road. The road is capable of accomodating camping trailers and other medium size RV units up to the Mono Creek Campground about five miles south of where the pavement ends. The remaining five miles to Crystal Park must be traveled over a very narrow, winding road with some steep sections, so it is advisable to leave camping units at the Mono Creek Campground or one of the other campsites down the valley. About .5 mile from the Mono Creek Campground there is a junction. Unless you plan to visit the Elkhorn Mining area, stay to the right. A drive of about 4.5 miles will bring you to Crystal Park, easily recognized by the fenced area, descriptive sign, and the telltale pits on the hillside.

It is hoped that those who visit Crystal Park will not abuse their privilege. Although there is evidence of littering and vandalism, the area is remarkably clean. A concerted effort on the part of those who visit here will insure a continuing source of fine crystal specimens for future generations.

Several areas other than Crystal Park itself are worth visiting. One of these is the Elkhorn Mining District east of Crystal Park. Mining activity began here in 1872 and continued sporadically up until 1930. Then during the early 1960s a few of the underground mines were worked again for several years. The predominantly silver-producing mines presently lie idle, but during the years of 1902 to 1965, they produced over $300,000 worth of silver, gold, copper, lead, and zinc. The area is not one of the better mineral collecting areas in Montana, but specimens of pyrite, sphalerite, some molybdenite, and apparently wolframite have been found on some of the mine dumps.

Five miles south of Crystal Park the road passes Elkhorn Hot Springs, a resort community where a plunge of geothermal waters is kept open most

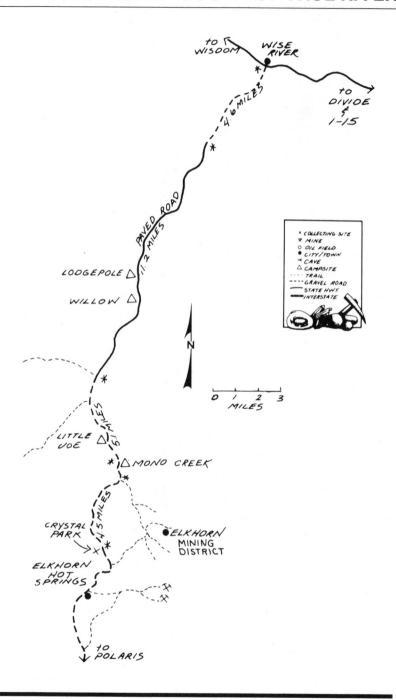

to WISDOM
WISE RIVER
to DIVIDE & I-15

4.6 MILES

PAVED ROAD
11.2 MILES

LOODGEPOLE △
WILLOW △

N

	COLLECTING SITE
✕	MINE
○	OIL FIELD
●	CITY/TOWN
	CAVE
△	CAMPSITE
	TRAIL
	GRAVEL ROAD
	STATE HWY.
	INTERSTATE

0 1 2 3
MILES

5.1 MILES

LITTLE JOE △
△ MONO CREEK

4.5 MILES

CRYSTAL PARK
● ELKHORN MINING DISTRICT

ELKHORN HOT SPRINGS

to POLARIS

of the year. Continuing an additional thirteen miles south of Elkhorn Hot Springs, one will encounter State Highway 278. From here, visits to the Big Hole Battlefield National Monument near Wisdom or the ghost town of Bannack, first territorial capital of Montana, are recommended.

Calvert Hill

The Calvert Hill region west of Wise River is noted for the large garnet and epidote crystals which can be found there. The area is reached by driving about six miles west of Wise River on Highway 43 to the campground near the Dickey Bridge. From there it is about another eight miles on a dirt and gravel road to the Calvert Hill area. The country rock contains considerable quantities of garnet and epidote therefore good specimens should be relatively easy to find.

Access Information: National Forest Service land, patented and unpatented
  mining claims in the Elkhorn Mining District.
Useful Maps: BLM Public Lands in Montana maps: 31 *Big Hole* and 32 *Dillon*.
U.S. Geological Survey *Maurice Mountain, Stine Mountain,* and *Wise River*.
  Quadrangles, Montana; 7.5 Minute Series, Topographic, scale 1:24,000.
U.S. Geological Survey *Polaris* and *Vipond Park* Quadrangles, Montana; 15
  Minute Series, Topographic scale, 1:62,500.
Specific References:
Geach, R. D. *Mines and Mineral Deposits (Except Fuels), Beaverhead County,
  Montana.* Montana Bureau of Mines and Geology Bulletin 85, pp. 104-110,
  1972.

The Butte Mining District

The story of the "Richest Hill on Earth" probably started with the intrusion of the Boulder Batholith, a granite-like mass formed about 60 million years ago. As hot solutions containing ore minerals penetrated fractures in the cooling batholith and in the surrounding Precambrian, Paleozoic, and Mesozoic sedimentary rocks, veins of rich ores were deposited. Exposed at the earth's surface by mountain building and erosional processes, the batholith and other rocks revealed their riches to prospectors and exploitation of the area began.

It was 1864 when gold was found in stream gravels along Silver Bow Creek, in what is now downtown Butte. Outcrops revealing ore-bearing veins were ultimately discovered, and hardrock mining was established. The mines were shallow at first, but soon depth was required to locate the valuable ore. The Mountain Con Mine, for example, was developed to a depth of 5,300 feet, a little more than one mile.

The passage of the Mining Law of May 10, 1872, provided miners the exclusive right to mine veins throughout their entire depth as long as those veins originated within their claimed area on the surface. Because the veins were not often vertical, they would extend beneath other miner's surface claims. Also, numerous faults were found which cut and offset veins, so tracing them beyond short distances became extremely difficult. Before long, miners were involved in legal disputes concerning their rights to a particular vein. The quality of some disputes in fact was questionable. Battles were literally fought over the confusing issue.

Two books of historical interest have been listed in Appendix A. They are *Underground Warfare at Butte,* by Reno H. Sales, and *The War of the Copper*

The Berkeley Pit — Butte, Montana.

Kings, by C. B. Glasscock. These historical accounts of Butte are highly recommended to the reader since they readily show the fascinating and often violent history of this famous mining area.

In 1956 an open pit replaced the large underground operations. Now a large chasm dominates the landscape on the northeast edge of Butte. Mining in the Butte area has ceased, at least for the time being, because of economic reasons. The Berkeley Pit is spectacular and a permanent viewing station has been constructed on its southern edge so that visitors can see and hear about the geology and the mining which has taken place here. The viewing stand is located at the east end of Park Street.

The ore that was being mined was primarily copper, but other metals (gold, silver, zinc, and manganese) were also present. As the pit deepened and widened, it encountered the shafts and tunnels of previous underground operations. The ore obtained in open pit fashion was generally very low grade, but because of lower operating costs, it was mined at a profit.

The underground mines of Butte have been the source of some extremely beautiful and rare mineral specimens. Although the mines themselves are not accessible, specimens of crystalline pyrite, quartz, covellite, digenite, enargite, and rhodochrosite, among others, can be purchased from local rock shops. An excellent collection of Butte minerals can be viewed at the Mineral Museum on the campus of Montana Tech at the west end of Park Street. For those who are curious about underground mining operations, the World Museum of Mining, west of the Montana Tech campus, is worth a visit. Both of these museums are briefly discussed later in the book.

As one drives around Butte, numerous old dumps and tailings can be seen. These have more than likely been thoroughly searched by collectors, but sometimes micromount quality specimens of pyrite and a few other minerals are still found. Some dumps are easily accessible, and some are strictly forbidden as the "Absolutely No Trespassing" signs indicate. Local rock dealers may be able to provide information concerning interesting areas around Butte which are not mentioned in this book.

Access Information: Private land, patented and unpatented mining claims.
Useful Maps: BLM Public Lands in Montana maps: 22 *Avon* and 32 *Dillon.*
U.S. Geological Survey *Butte North* and *Butte South* Quadrangles, Montana;
  7.5 Minute Series, Topographic, scale 1:24,000.
Specific References:
Perry, E. S. "The Butte Mining District." *Billings Geological Society 1st Annual Field Conference Guidebook,* pp. 66-68, 1950.
Miller, R. N., Ed. *Guidebook for the Butte Field Meeting.* Society of Economic Geologists, 1973.
Weed, W. H. *Geology and Ore Deposits of the Butte District, Montana.* U.S. Geological Survey Professional Paper 74, 1912.

Minerals Near Butte

The rocks in the Radar Creek area between Toll Mountain and Interstate 90 have produced some of the finest smoky quartz crystals found anywhere. The crystals occur in pockets (miarolitic cavities) throughout the granite-like rocks of the Boulder Batholith, which is exposed in this region. The area is a popular one for local rockhounds and any material lying free on the surface has more than likely been picked up. Digging is perhaps the only way one will obtain good smoky quartz here, but it would help to seek additional information from local rockshops or rock club members as to its availability.

The Toll Mountain Campground has been the source of some large specimens of limonite pseudomorphs after pyrite. Cubes up to two inches across have been reported near the campground. The writer searched for some time without success to locate a specimen. Apparently, like many mineral occurrences, it has been well documented, but considerable time, patience and skill are required to find specimens.

The Pohndorf Amethyst Mine northeast of the campground is on private land, and because of the reputation of the mine for producing some very fine gem quality amethyst, access is not guaranteed. The early history of the mine centers around the operations of a Mr. Pohndorf who was a mineral dealer and jeweler from Denver. The amethyst crystals were found associated with tourmalinated quartz in a vuggy pegmatite. The quartz was, for the most part, poorly formed and the amethyst crystals were generally small. The amethyst was also not abundant nor was all of it gem quality. Though reports indicate more gem quality amethyst could be recovered, considerable quantities of rock would have to be removed, making the operation not economically feasible at this time. Some very fine amethyst "scepter" crystals from the Pohndorf Mine and other excellent crystal groups from adjacent areas can be viewed at the Mineral Museum of Montana Tech and several rock shops in Butte.

As mentioned earlier, the granite-like rocks of the Boulder Batholith east of Butte often possess miarolitic cavities containing quartz crystals. Several pegmatites with quartz crystal-lined vugs outcrop along the north shore of Delmoe Lake. The action of waves upon these rocks apparently breaks the crystals loose and they can periodically be found in the sand and gravel along the shore during periods of low water. The crystals to be found are not necessarily large, but they often possess nice terminations. The shoreline in

MINERALS EAST OF BUTTE

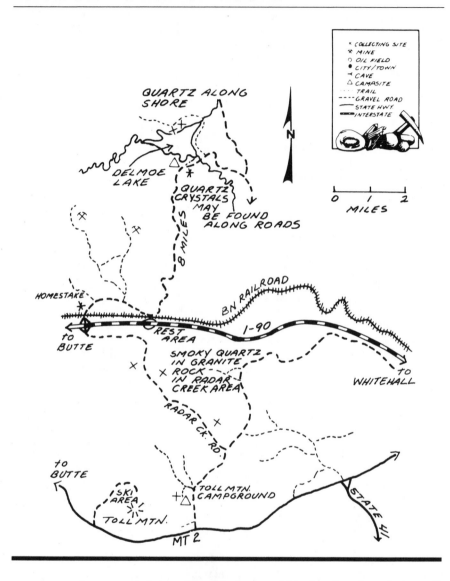

QUARTZ ALONG SHORE

DELMOE LAKE

QUARTZ CRYSTALS MAY BE FOUND ALONG ROADS

8 MILES

N

COLLECTING SITE
MINE
OIL FIELD
CITY/TOWN
CAVE
CAMPSITE
TRAIL
GRAVEL ROAD
STATE HWY.
INTERSTATE

0   1   2
MILES

HOMESTAKE

BN RAILROAD

REST AREA

I-90

TO BUTTE

SMOKY QUARTZ IN GRANITE
ROCK IN RADAR CREEK AREA

TO WHITEHALL

RADAR CK. RD.

TO BUTTE

SKI AREA

TOLL MTN.

TOLL MTN. CAMPGROUND

STATE 41

MT 2

some areas shows some interesting thin layers of black colored sand. A small magnet immediately shows the sand to be composed of tiny grains of the mineral magnetite. If you have a small magnet with you and visit the area, be sure to keep a piece of paper between the magnet and the magnetite sand grains or you may have difficulty cleaning the magnet.

Rocks in the immediate vicinity of Delmoe Lake have been known to produce small crystals of sphene and pyrite in small cavities, and quartz crystals can sometimes be found along roads between the lake and Interstate 90.

Access Information: Private land, National Forest land, patented and unpatented mining claims.
Useful Maps: BLM Public Lands in Montana map: 32 *Dillon.* U.S. Geological Survey *Delmoe Lake, Grace, Homestake,* and *Pipestone Pass* Quadrangles, Montana; 7.5 Minute Series, Topographic, scale 1:24,000.
U.S. Geological Survey *Basin* and *Elk Park* Quadrangles, Montana; 15 Minute Series, Topographic, scale 1:62,500.
Specific References:
Heinrich, E. W. *Pegamite Mineral Deposits in Montana.* Montana Bureau of Mines and Geology Memoir 28, 1948.
Miller, R. N., Ed. *Guidebook for the Butte Field Meeting.* Society of Economic Geologists, 1973.

Anaconda Area

For many years, the smelter at Anaconda treated the ores of the Butte Mining District. Large quantities of ore were processed here, as evidenced by the tremendous tailings and slag piles to the east of town. The operation here was stupendous, and one of the more noticeable landmarks of this community is the giant smoke stack high on the hill south of town. It is a major feature in the landscape and can be seen from a considerable distance. The apparent low price of copper and increasing mining costs recently forced ARCO to curb its activities in Butte. Ore was no longer being shipped to the smelter in Anaconda and eventually the smelter ceased operations. This was soon followed by a closure of the famous Berkeley Pit in Butte. The huge smelter in Anaconda has been dismantled, and the large smoke stack may someday be reduced to rubble.

Several mining districts exist adjacent to the Deer Lodge Valley north of Anaconda, but only one of them was of any consequence. The Zosell or Emery Mining District is located about seven miles east of Deer Lodge and lies in low mountain country. Several maintained gravel roads provide access to the region.

Mining in the Zosell District first took place in 1872 when placer gold was discovered. This was followed by the mining of lode deposits in 1887, and by the late 1920s nearly three quarters of a million dollars in gold, silver, and lead had been produced.

The rocks which contained the metalliferous deposits are Late Cretaceous volcanic rocks, possibly related to the intrusion of the nearby Boulder Batholith. A study of the mineralogy expressed by the various ore bodies in the district reveals that they are relatively complex. If accessible, the mine dumps and tailings may produce specimens of arsenopyrite, pyrite, sphalerite, galena, chalcopyrite, and quartz.

Immediately to the south of the Zosell District along Dry Cottonwood Creek, sapphires of both gem and abrasive quality were discovered in placer deposits which were worked in the early 1900s. These deposits have been worked intermittently, and no significant mining is taking place here at the present. The source of the sapphires found in Dry Cottonwood Creek has not yet been determined. It is assumed, however, that they originated from igneous intrusions, much like the other gem corundum deposits found in Montana.

A small pegmatite containing the blue-green microcline variety amazonstone occurs about three miles due north of Anaconda on Lost Creek. The pegmatite is unique because of its scenic occurrence. It is located at the base of a water-

The huge smokestack at Anaconda is a landmark.

fall and along the valley's north wall. It is associated with a relatively small granitic intrusion of Late Cretaceous age. Other small pegmatite sills crop out in the area, and these contain an assortment of minerals, none existing as nice euhedral crystals, however.

It is suggested that, since the deposits of amazonstone are limited and primarily found within the confines of a state park, rockhounds refrain from collecting here. It may be best to preserve this deposit and regard it as one which should only be observed and not exploited.

One of Montana's earlier mining regions lies about fifteen miles west of Anaconda on Montana Highway 1. Since the operation of the Georgetown Placer in 1865, this area adjacent to Georgetown Lake was noted as a major gold producer. It is presently used for recreation—boating, water sports, and fishing—and the Cable Mountain area to the northeast has been developed for winter sports such as skiing and snowmobiling. The ghost town of Cable lies here and evidence of past lode mining is apparent in the form of many mine dumps and tailings adjacent to the old community. There may be in them some mineral specimens for the collector, but most likely just common sulfides. Several tungsten prospects have been located here, and a few have been mined, yielding fair quantities of ore. The tungsten mineral present is scheelite, and searching for it at night with a short-wave ultraviolet light should reveal its brilliant blue-white fluorescence. Some pale green to dark green epidote crystals are occasionally associated with the scheelite, contained in pieces of rock that are generally attractive and often suitable as cabinet specimens.

West of Georgetown Lake, MT Highway 1 descends to the Flint Creek Valley through a deep, narrow canyon. Steeply tilted rock layers of Precambrian Belt Series argillites and quartzites help to make this a spectacular route to the Philipsburg area. The rock layers along the road can provide rockhounds with examples of many shallow water sedimentary features such as ripple marks,

ZOSELL (EMERY) DISTRICT

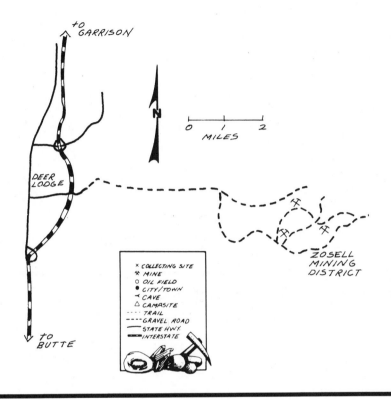

mud cracks, and rare raindrop impressions. Care should be taken, though, since the steep slopes and cliffs are subject to landslides and rockfalls.

Access Information: Private land, patented and unpatented mining claims, National Forest Service land.

Useful Maps: BLM Public Lands in Montana map: 21 *Granite*.

U.S. Geological Survey *Georgetown Lake, Silver Lake,* and *West Valley* Quadrangles, Montana; 7.5 Minute Series, Topographic, scale 1:24,000.

U.S. Geological Survey *Anaconda* and *Deer Lodge* Quadrangles, Montana; 15 Minute Series, Topographic, scale 1:62,500.

Specific References:

Clabaugh, S. E. *Corundum Deposits in Montana.* U.S. Geological Survey Bulletin 983, pp. 52-54, 1952.

LOST CREEK FALLS AMAZONSTONE

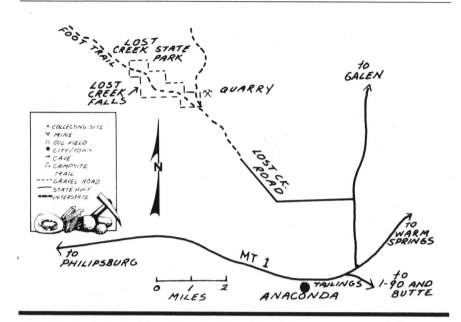

FOOT TRAIL

LOST CREEK STATE PARK

LOST CREEK FALLS

QUARRY

to GALEN

LOST CK. ROAD

× COLLECTING SITE
✷ MINE
○ OIL FIELD
● CITY/TOWN
⌐ CAVE
△ CAMPSITE
--- TRAIL
----- GRAVEL ROAD
—— STATE HWY
▬▬ INTERSTATE

N

to WARM SPRINGS

to PHILIPSBURG

MT 1

0 1 2
MILES

ANACONDA

TAILINGS

to I-90 AND BUTTE

GEORGETOWN-CABLE AREA

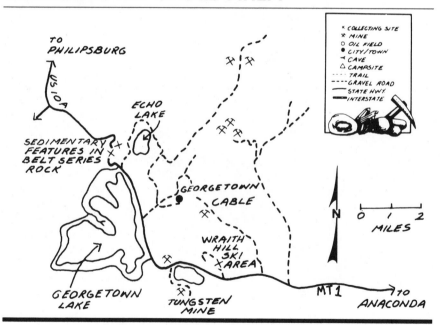

TO PHILIPSBURG

US 10A

ECHO LAKE

SEDIMENTARY FEATURES IN BELT SERIES ROCK

× COLLECTING SITE
✷ MINE
○ OIL FIELD
● CITY/TOWN
⌐ CAVE
△ CAMPSITE
--- TRAIL
----- GRAVEL ROAD
—— STATE HWY
▬▬ INTERSTATE

GEORGETOWN CABLE

N

0 1 2
MILES

WRAITH HILL SKI AREA

GEORGETOWN LAKE

TUNGSTEN MINE

MT 1

to ANACONDA

Earll, F. N. *Mines and Mineral Deposits of the Southern Flint Creek Range, Montana.* Montana Bureau of Mines and Geology Bulletin 84, 1972.

Poulter, C. J. *Geology of the Georgetown Thrust Area Southwest of Philipsburg, Granite and Deer Lodge Counties, Montana.* Montana Bureau of Mines and Geology Geologic Map Series GM-I, 1957.

Robertson, Forbes. *Geology and Mineral Deposits of the Zosell (Emery) Mining District, Powell County, Montana.* Montana Bureau of Mines and Geology Memoir 34, 1953.

Philipsburg Area

The Philipsburg District was a relatively important one during the early 1900s, after the discovery of gold and silver near Georgetown to the south. Several deposits have been exploited in the district and the presence of a smelter, of which only twin smokestacks remain, indicates an extensive source of ore.

The occurrence of minerals like pyrolusite, psilomelane, and rhodochrosite attest to the fact that manganese was one of the major elements being searched for here. Fragments of the host rock are common on the dumps and tailing, and cavities or vugs in this rock may reveal outstanding tiny crystals of manganese minerals. The possibility of obtaining some interesting micromount specimens in this area is good.

Several of the mines have been reactivated for their gold and silver potential. Although they are expensive ventures, the increased price of gold and new mining techniques may allow profit. The fact that there are active mines present in the region makes it even more necessary to obtain permission before collecting from what appear to be abandoned mines.

About four miles east of Philipsburg are the remains of one of the more colorful mining camps of Montana's past. What is left of this community lies

Mine dumps, tailings, and collapsing structures near Philipsburg.

on the edge of an open meadow near the crest of a mountain ridge. The ghost town of Granite is reached by a steep, narrow and rocky road which winds its way around the mountainside. Exercise extreme caution and watch for oncoming vehicles while driving this route. The trip is worthwhile, however, since it provides not only access to a famous historic site, but also access to many scenic overlooks from which some spectacular mountain country can be viewed.

Access Information: Private land, patented and unpatented mining claims, National Forest Service land.

Useful Maps: BLM Public Lands in Montana map: 21 *Granite.*

U.S. Geological Survey *Fred Burr Lake, Henderson Mountain, Maxville,* and *Philipsburg* Quadrangles, Montana; 7.5 Minute Series, Topographic, scale 1:24,000.

Specific References:

Emmons, W. H., and Calkins, F. C. *Geology and Ore Deposits of the Philipsburg Quadrangle, Montana.* U.S. Geological Survey Professional Paper 78, 1913.

Prinz, W. C. *Geology and Ore Deposits of the Philipsburg District, Granite County, Montana.* U.S. Geological Survey Bulletin 1237, 1967.

PHILIPSBURG AREA

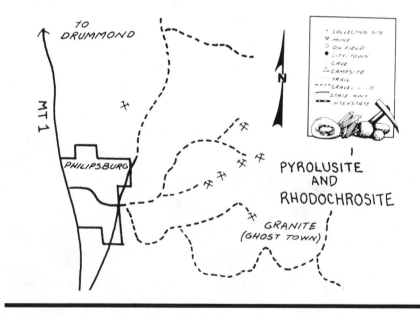

Gem Mountain Sapphire Mine

The sapphire deposits at the Gem Mountain locality are somewhat similar to those in the Helena area, but they were not deposited by a stream the size of the Missouri River. These deposits include bench and terrace gravels which were laid down by mountain streams. Also, unlike the Helena deposits the possible source of the sapphires has not yet been found. Some igneous rocks in the gravels contain sapphires, and therefore their origin may at least be similar to those of the Helena region. It has been reported though, that the sapphires found at Gem Mountain exhibit a much wider range of color (from yellow to pink and lavender) than those found at other localities in the state.

As of last report, there is no fee digging at Gem Mountain, but customers may purchase buckets of unscreened and unprocessed gravel from the mine and have mine workers wash the gravel for them. Bags of pre-screened "paydirt" concentrate are available for purchase in case customers are interested in looking for sapphires in the comfort of their own home. The owners of the mine also provide a faceting service and offer classes in the art of faceting and setting gemstones. Camping facilities are located at the mine with fresh water available, but no electrical hookups.

The mine is open from Memorial Day through the Sunday following Labor Day, 9:00 a.m. to 6:00 p.m., and can be reached by driving six miles south of Philipsburg on MT Highway 1 to Route 38, then an additional seventeen miles west of this junction. It can also be reached from Hamilton by driving east

GEM MOUNTAIN SAPPHIRE MINE

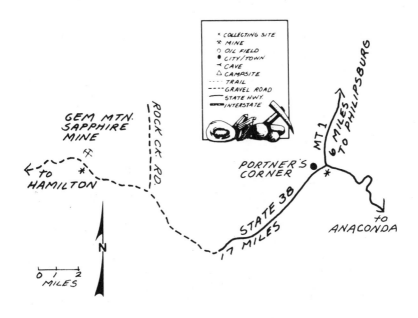

on Route 38, but sections of this road may be impassable during the early spring or late fall.

For more information, write or call:

Gem Mountain Sapphire Mine
P.O. Box 701
Philipsburg, MT 59858
(406) 859-3530

Access Information: Private land, patented and unpatented mining claims, National Forest Service Land.
Useful Maps: BLM Public Lands in Montana map: 21 *Granite.*
U.S. Geological Survey *Cornish Gulch, Maukey Gulch, Mt. Ermerine,* and *Stony Creek* Quadrangles, Montana: 7.5 Minute Series, Topographic, scale 1:24,000.
Specific References:
Badgely, Kirk Jr. "Rock Creek Sapphire Placers." *Billings Geological Society 16th Annual Field Conference Guidebook,* pp. 120-121, 1965.
Clabaugh, S.E. *Corundum Deposits of Montana.* U.S. Geological Survey Bulletin No. 983, pp. 145-52, 1952.

Drummond Area

The geology around Drummond is quite complex. Rocks have been subjected to daistrophic forces, and strata of many ages are exposed over short distances.

Fossil leaves can be found in Mid-Tertiary rocks northeast of Drummond. From the east end of town, follow the Helmville Road in order to reach the localities. About six miles must be traveled before several road cuts expose the fossiliferous strata. Extremely well preserved leaves, insects, and a few rare fish skeletons have been reported, but diligent searching is now required in order to find good specimens. The talus slopes below the exposures are usually good places to search.

A railroad cut about 4.5 miles west of Drummond exposes some steeply tilted rock layers of Jurassic and Cretaceous age. The marine layers of the Jurassic rocks have produced some fairly well preserved fossils. Several species of mollusks have been reported from the Rierdon and Sawtooth shales and limestones present near the east end of the railroad cut. A species of the oyster *Gryphaea* is one of the more common fossils to be found here.

Part of the Lower Cretaceous Kootenai Formation, exposed as limestone ridges nearby, is composed of abundant fossil snail shells. It is commonly referred to as the "Gastropod Limestone" by geologists and is a very useful rock unit when geologic mapping is conducted in Cretaceous rocks of western Montana. The snails are fresh water types of several species and apparently lived in a large lake that occupied a good portion of western Montana during the Early Cretaceous Period.

Paleozoic limestones, located a few miles up Rattler Gulch to the north, have been quarried as a source of calcium. The Late Paleozoic rocks exposed here are also sources of fossils, best found where they many montain roads cut through upturned rock layers.

Dredge tailings along Bearcreek between I-90 and Garnet tell of an era when "gold fever" existed in western Montana.

Calcite crystals, a "vuggy" travertine, and calcareous tufa can be found near old U.S. Highway 10 north of Interstate 90 about 5.5 miles east of the Bearmouth Chalet Motel. The calcite crystals are found in the reddish or pink rocks on the slopes between the old highway and the Clark Fork River. The best collecting is generally near the bottom of the slope close to the river. Caution must be exercised—the slope is very steep and the rocks on it are loose.

About ten miles west of Drummond on old U.S. Highway 10 there are the huge dredge tailings in Bear Gulch. These tailings of early gold placer operations are easily visible as one travels northward from the highway along Bear Creek. Initially developed in 1865, the gravels produced close to 7 million dollars in gold and silver within a fifty-year time span.

Five major mining districts operated in the area north of Bearmouth. Several communities arose as a result of the ambitious mining efforts but declined rapidly as production of minerals decreased. The ruins of these old towns still exist today as testimony of the mining activities of bygone days.

Beartown represented the center of the Bear Creek Placer District between Bearmouth and Garnet. The First Chance District, centered around the town of Garnet, was the most important of the lode mining districts in the area because it produced more than 3.5 million dollars worth of gold, silver, copper, lead, and zinc between the years of 1867 and 1955. The old ghost town of Garnet is presently being restored (the restoration project was initiated by several federal agencies, but is apparently becoming more dependent upon volunteer help and related monetary aid). The Coloma District lies about two miles northwest of Garnet, and though the mineralization here is similar to that at Garnet, only $450,000 worth of ore was produced as of 1960. The remaining two districts, The Copper Cliff and Top O'Deep, were

DRUMMOND AND GARNET AREA

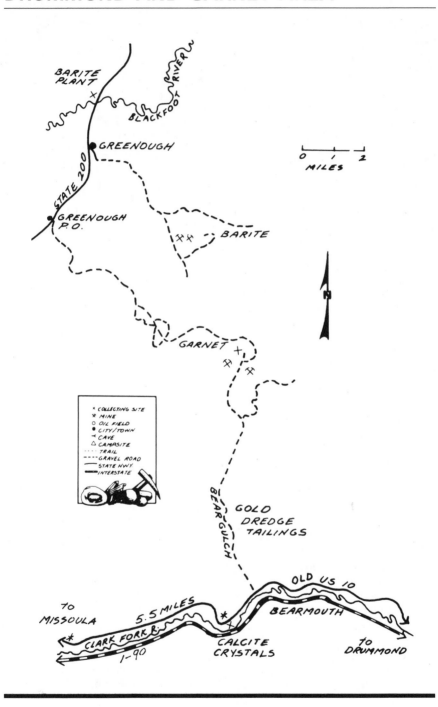

BARITE PLANT

BLACKFOOT RIVER

GREENOUGH

STATE 200

GREENOUGH P.O.

BARITE

N

GARNET

× COLLECTING SITE
✶ MINE
○ OIL FIELD
● CITY/TOWN
◄ CAVE
△ CAMPSITE
.... TRAIL
------- GRAVEL ROAD
——— STATE HWY.
━━━ INTERSTATE

0   1   2
MILES

BEAR GULCH

GOLD DREDGE TAILINGS

OLD US 10

TO MISSOULA

5.5 MILES

BEARMOUTH

CLARK FORK R.

I-90

CALCITE CRYSTALS

TO DRUMMOND

DRUMMOND AREA

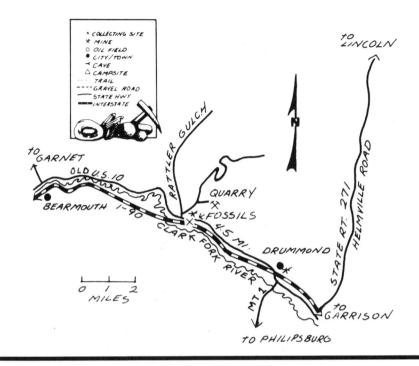

producers on a much smaller scale. The total production between them to date has been about $75,000.

The ore bodies resulted from replacement processes and deposition by metalliferous solutions in sedimentary and igneous rocks. It is obvious that the rich placer deposits originated from the erosion of lode deposits near the heads of the streams. Gold then, can perhaps still be found in the gravels of the many streams in the area, and panning the gravels may produce a little color. If you do plan to hobby pan for gold here, be certain of land status before doing so. Many of the streams are protected by mining claims.

Fossils may be found in outcrops of Paleozoic limestone along roadways in the region. Brachiopods, bryozoans, corals, and crinoid remains will be most common. Relatively complete faunal lists for the various rock units are presented in Montana Bureau of Mines and Geology Memoir 39.

Massive Barite, mostly gray-white in color, occurs in veins north and west of Garnet. Although these occurrences are fairly wide spread and have been well documented, only one area has been mined extensively since their initial discovery. A major deposit located about five miles southeast of the community of Greenough has been mined since the early 1950s, and ore has been shipped to a mill adjacent to State Highway 200 along the Blackfoot River. The barite occurs as vein-like bodies in Precambrian Belt Series quartzites and argillites.

Some pyrite, galena, and sphalerite is associated with some deposits, but the presence of these minerals is apparently insignificant.

Access Information: Private land, BLM land, patented and unpatented mining claims.

Useful Maps: BLM Public Lands in Montana map: 21 *Granite.* U.S. Geological Survey *Bata Mtn., Browns Lake, Chamberlain Mtn., Chimney Lakes, Elevation Mtn., Greenough, Helmville, Union Peak,* and *Wild Horse Parks* Quadrangles, Montana; 7.5 Minute Series, Topographic, scale 1:24,000.

U.S. Geological Survey *Bearmouth* and *Drummond* Quadrangles, Montana; 15 Minute Series, Topographic, scale 1:62,500.

USDA Forest Service Visitors Map; Lolo National Forest, Idaho and Montana.

Specific References: DeMunck, V. C., and Ackerman, W. C. *Barite Deposits in Montana.* Montana Bureau of Mines and Geology Information Circular 22, pp. 13-17, 1958.

Gwinn, V. E. *Geology of the Drummond Area, Central-Western Montana.* Montana Bureau of Mines and Geology Special Publication 21 (Geologic Map No. 4), 1961.

Kauffman, M. E. *Geology of the Garnet-Bearmouth Area, Western Montana.* Montana Bureau of Mines and Geology Memoir 39, 1963.

Landreth, J. O. *High Calcium Limestone Deposit in the Rattler Gulch Area, Granite County, Montana.* Montana Bureau of Mines and Geology Special Publication 44, 1968.

Miller, M. R. *Guidebook of the Drummond-Elkhorn Areas, West-Central Montana* (2nd Ed.). Montana Bureau of Mines and Geology Special Publication 82, pp. 11-16, 1980.

Winston, Don. "Second Day Geologic Road Log, Philipsburg-Drummond-Galen." *Billings Geological Society 16th Annual Field Conference Guidebook,* pp. 164-167, 1965.

Yen, T. C. *Fresh-water Mollusks of Cretaceous Age from Montana and Wyoming.* U.S. Geological Survey Professional Paper 233-A, 1951.

Clinton Mining District

The Clinton Mining District lies about two miles northeast of the small town of the same name. Since their discovery in 1878, the ore deposits have provided close to $100,000 in copper, silver, lead, and gold.

Mineralization occurred in the Early Tertiary Period when pre-existing Precambrian metamorphic and Late Cretaceous plutonic rocks were subjected to fracturing. The fractures were subsequently filled with ore minerals.

Lying on the south slopes of the Garnet Range, the district is reached by a scenic mountain road leading north from Clinton. Several mines are present, a few of them lying at a relatively low elevation. Since some have operated fairly recently, their dumps and tailings have not yet been deeply weathered. These areas, therefore, have the potential of providing examples of several different minerals. Small cavities in the rocks on the mine dumps will sometimes contain nicely formed crystals. These specimens would be useful for micromount collections. The writer had the opportunity some years ago to view a small collection of microminerals from this area, and they were fairly impressive. If access is gained to the mine dumps, search for chalcopyrite, tetrahedrite, galena, pyrite, bornite, barite, siderite, hematite, calcite, and quartz.

CLINTON MINING DISTRICT

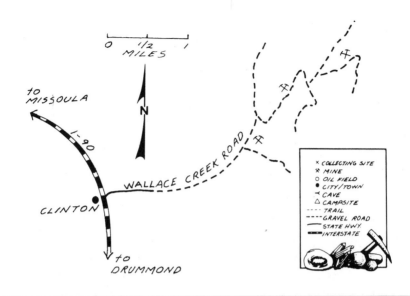

Access Information: Private land, patented and unpatented mining claims, BLM land.

Useful Maps: BLM Public Lands in Montana map: 21 *Granite.* U.S. Geological Survey *Clinton* and *Mineral Ridge* Quadrangles, Montana; 7.5 Minute Series, Topographic, scale 1:24,000.

USDA Forest Service Forest Visitors Map; Lolo National Forest, Idaho and Montana.

Specific Information:

Hintzman, D. E. *Geology and Ore Deposits of the Clinton Mining District, Missoula County, Montana.* Montana Bureau of Mines and Geology Bulletin 40, 1964.

Sahinen, U. M. *Mines and Mineral Deposits, Missoula and Ravalli Counties, Montana.* Montana Bureau of Mines and Geology Bulletin 8, pp. 32-37, 1975.

Hamilton Area

Several small mining districts are located west and northwest of Victor. The most predominant of these is the Curlew District where lead and silver were the major metals produced.

Mining activity began about 1887 and continued intermittently until fairly recently. Several hundred thousand dollars worth of silver, lead, gold, copper, and zinc were removed.

The primary ore mineral occurring in the Curlew Mine appears to be argentiferous galena. Specimens can frequently be found on the mine dumps and tailings, but good crystals are rare. The mineralization of the region is not well understood since the records kept were poor. It appears, though, that most of the ore deposits may occur as the result of contact metamorphism or as

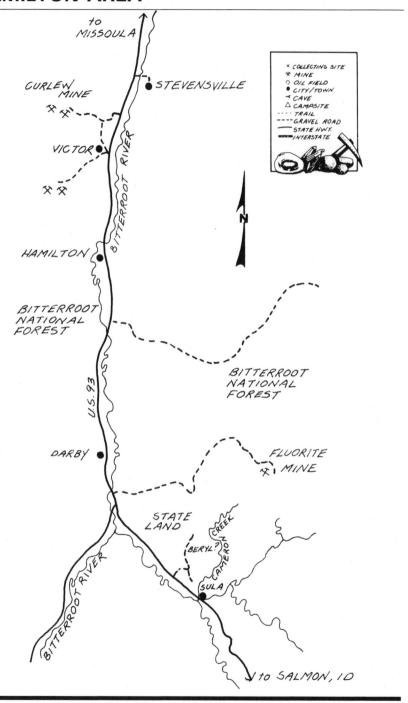

to
MISSOULA

STEVENSVILLE

CURLEW
MINE

VICTOR

BITTERROOT RIVER

HAMILTON

BITTERROOT
NATIONAL
FOREST

U.S. 93

DARBY

BITTERROOT
NATIONAL
FOREST

FLUORITE
MINE

STATE
LAND

CAMERON CREEK

BERYL?

SULA

BITTERROOT RIVER

to SALMON, ID

X COLLECTING SITE
✴ MINE
○ OIL FIELD
● CITY/TOWN
◄ CAVE
△ CAMPSITE
------ TRAIL
- - - - GRAVEL ROAD
――― STATE HWY.
▬▬▬ INTERSTATE

N

hydrothermal deposition along faults. More than likely, the mineralization in the district is related, at least to some degree, to the intrusion of the Idaho Batholith, a granite-like body which lies just to the west.

The mines are accessible by dirt and gravel roads leading west from Victor, but care should be taken when and where the roads may be wet.

On the east side of the valley adjacent to Victor several exposures of the indurated volcanic ash called pumicite will occasionally produce some very unique and unusually formed concretions. The more interesting of these are the ones which consist of a multiple of nodules. The outcrops containing the concretions are recognized by their light color as opposed to the darker rock types more common in the region.

Several deposits containing the mineral fluorite have been located about twenty-six miles east of Darby, but access to them is uncertain. The fluorite is high grade and occurs as white, green, and deep purple masses. The grains are relatively small, less than one inch in diameter on the average, making it quite unlike the popular cleavable fluorite from Illinois. Small piles of fluorite can periodically be found along the road between Darby and the fluorite deposits, probably material which fell from the trucks hauling ore to Darby for shipment. Since the deposits are possibly inaccessible, one could probably look for specimens here.

The fluorite deposits occur in igneous and metamorphic rocks and may be related to the Idaho Batholith as far as origin is concerned. The mineral is found as lenses within the surrounding rock and was exposed in relatively large amounts at the surface. The lenses were discovered in 1937 during the construction of a Forest Service trail, but mining of the mineral did not begin until the early 1950s. Mining was open pit and development of the mines has continued up to the present.

About 2.5 miles north of Sula, beryl was discovered in a pegmatite dike which was exposed during logging operations in 1954. The beryl, which was easily available, was quickly collected by specimen hunters and, although other deposits have since been discovered, they are certainly not common and are difficult to locate. Specimens found were light green to blue-green in color and were not of gem quality. Apparently they existed as nice euhedral crystals ranging in size from needle-like to varying fractions of an inch in thickness and length. Large scale mining operations have not taken place because the quantity of beryl has been estimated to be insufficient to support such operations.

Access Information: Private land, National Forest Service land, patented and unpatented mining claims.

Useful Maps: U.S. Geological Survey *Bald Top Mountain, Darby, Deer Mtn., French Basin, Robbins Gulch, Sula,* and *Victor* Quadrangles, Montana; 7.5 Minute Series, Topographic, scale 1.24,000.

USDA Forest Service Forest Visitors Map; Bitterroot National Forest; Idaho and Montana.

Specific References:

Ross, C. P. *Fluorspar Prospects in Montana.* U.S. Geological Survey Bulletin 955-E, 1950.

Sahinen, U. M. *Mines and Mineral Deposits, Missoula and Ravalli Counties, Montana.* Montana Bureau of Mines and Geology Bulletin 8, pp. 55-57, 1957.

Sahinen, U. M. *Fluorspar Deposits in Montana*. Montana Bureau of Mines and
Geology Bulletin 28, pp. 5-11, 1962.

Quartz Crystals Near Lolo Hot Springs

In the area north and west of Lolo Hot Springs, along Granite Creek and
its tributaries, numerous outcrops of the granitic Idaho Batholith are accessible because of extensive logging. Crystals of clear to very dark smoky quartz
can be found in miarolitic cavities within the rock and sometimes they are
even found loose in the soil. Their occurrence is somewhat similar to that
at Crystal Park south of Wise River.

In order to locate areas where quartz crystals may occur, carefully examine
the rock exposures in road cuts, hillsides, and regions of recent logging. In
particular, look for patches of smoky quartz or the presence of unusually large
grains of quartz and feldspar (pegmatite). Most of the rock in the area is
generally uniform in texture, with relatively small grains of quartz and feldspar,
and so the pegmatite nature of a rock outcrop may indicate a potential source
of well formed crystals.

Extreme care should be taken in extracting the crystals. Many beautiful
specimens have been destroyed by hasty decisions and poor judgment in

QUARTZ CRYSTALS AT
LOLO HOT SPRINGS AREA

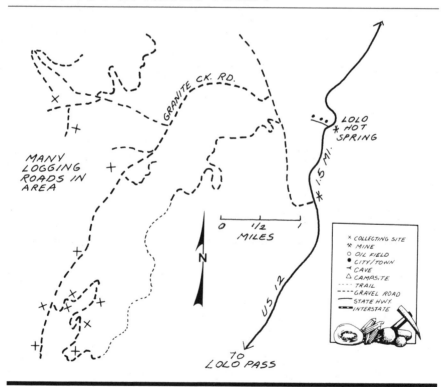

removing them from the host rock. Groups of brilliant crystals of various size can often be the prize of the patient collector.

There is a mining claim here where quartz crystals are being mined commercially, so be sure to honor all "No Trespassing" signs.

The general collecting area can be reached by the Granite Creek road, which leaves U.S. Highway 12 about 1.5 miles south of Lolo Hot Springs. There are many logging roads here so a current forest service map (available at the Federal Building in Missoula) can be helpful.

Several small mines can be found along U.S. Highway 12 between Lolo Hot Springs and the community of Lolo to the east. Mine records indicate small (if any) shipments of copper and silver ore. Dumps and tailings will probably yield little of interest to the collector except possibly some pyrite, galena, chalcopyrite, and copper carbonate minerals.

Lolo Hot Springs is a natural source of geothermal water. It has been developed into a resort and provides weary vacationers with relaxation and comfortably warm water in a well kept pool.

Access Information: National Forest Service land, patented and unpatented mining claims, private land.
Useful Maps: U.S. Geological Survey *Lolo Hot Springs* Quadrangle, Montana; 7.5 Minutes Series, Topographic, scale 1:24,000.
USDA Forest Service Visitors Map; Lolo National Forest, Idaho and Montana.

Specific References:
Sahinen, U. M. *Mines and Mineral Deposits, Missoula and Ravalli Counties, Montana.* Montana Bureau of Mines and Geology Bulletin 8, pp. 39-40, 1957.

Fossils North of Missoula

During the Tertiary Period relatively large lakes occupied the Missoula Valley and others nearby. Sediments, including volcanic dust and silt accumulated in these lake basins, eventually producing a rock called pumicite. As these sediments were being deposited, plant remains were buried and preserved. Today the outcrops of pumicite are often sources of beatifully preserved fossil leaf prints. In most areas along the valley margins where pumicite (recognized by its whitish color) outcrops, fossil leaf prints can be found by splitting the rock along bedding planes. The varying degrees of hardness demonstrated by this rock makes the revealing of complete leaf prints somewhat of a challenge.

North of Missoula there are several coal mines, operated intermittently from the 1890s to the mid 1900s, which produced a fair amount of lignite coal. Pumicite is exposed on the dumps, which offer the potential of some fine fossil leaf prints. Specimens of the genera *Sequoia, Glyplostrobus, Alnus, Carpinus, Cornusor, Viburnum, Populus,* and *Taxodium* have been reported. The specimens are normally very fragile when first exposed and should dry thoroughly before being handled. Good specimens are easily destroyed by the impatient collector.

Access Information: Private land, patented and unpatented mining claims.
Useful Maps: U.S. Geological Survey *Northwest Missoula* Quadrangle, Montana; 7.5 Minute Series, Topographic, scale 1:24,000.
USDA Forest Service Forest Visitors Map; *Lolo National Forest, Idaho* and *Montana.*

FOSSILS NORTH OF MISSOULA

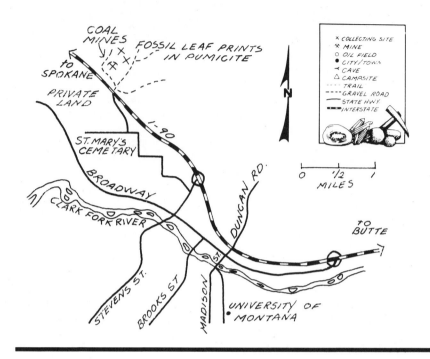

Specific References:

Rowe, J. P. *Some Volcanic Ash Beds of Montana.* Montana University Bulletin 17, Geol. Ser. No. 1, 1903.

Sahinen, U. M. *Mines and Mineral Deposits, Missoula and Ravalli Counties, Montana.* Montana Bureau of Mines and Geology Bulletin 8, pp. 44-46, 1957.

Superior-St. Regis Area

Considerable quantities of zinc, lead, copper, silver, and some gold have been recovered from the Superior-St. Regis area of western Montana during the past eighty years. The ores were found in veins associated with several major fault zones. The majority of the rocks occurring here are metamorphic types of the Precambrian Belt Series. Some younger igneous intrusions also occur throughout the area. Many of the mineral deposits which have been mined can generally be traced into the Coeur d'Alene District in Idaho just to the west.

A fair number of mines exist along the tributaries of the Clark Fork River to the north and south of Superior and St. Regis. Most of the major zinc, lead, and silver producing mines are found north of the Clark Fork River valley, while those which produced copper lie primarily to the south.

There are also several fluorite deposits. In fact, the first commercial production of fluorite in the state came from southwest of Superior. The fluorite has been found in several zones within Precambrian quartzites and argillites. It

SUPERIOR-ST. REGIS AREA

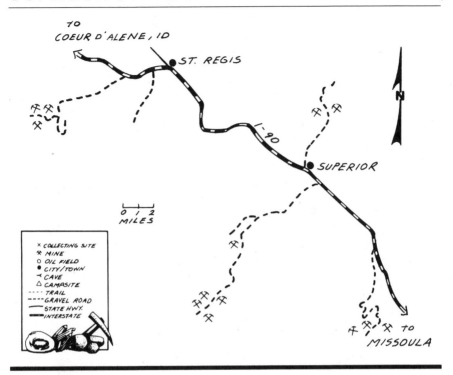

is generally fine-grained and no well-formed crystals have been reported.

Mineral collecting here would more than likely be confined to the many mine dumps and tailings, but local inquiry should be made regarding the status of the mines. The Wallace, Idaho, area to the west is a famous silver producing region, and therefore the mines in the Superior-St. Regis area may be considered to have similar potential. Claimholders may be reluctant to allow even the collecting of non-commercial minerals from their property.

Access Information: Private land, patented and unpatented mining claim, National Forest Service land.

Useful Maps: U.S. Geological Survey *Haugan, Illinois Peak, Plains, St. Regis,* and *Superior* Quadrangles, Montana; 15 Minute Series, Topographic, scale 1:62,500.

USDA Forest Service Forest Visitors Map; Lolo National Forest, Idaho and Montana.

Specific References:

Campbell, A. B. *Geology and Mineral Deposits of the St. Regis-Superior Area, Mineral County, Montana.* U.S. Geological Survey Bulletin 1082-T, 1960.

Thompson Falls Area

Numerous mines and old placer operations can be found near Thompson Falls along the many tributaries of the Clark Fork River. The earliest probably began in the early 1880s, during the Coeur d'Alene gold rush. Little is known concerning production then, but it is certain that fair quantities of gold were recovered from placer deposits. With the prospectors, however, came the enterprising businessmen who were more than willing to relieve the hard working miners of their short-lived wealth. Much of what was mined during the early history of the region was never recorded, but this is probably true of mining districts throughout Montana.

Though numerous mining districts can be found within Sanders County, those in the immediate vicinity of Thompson Falls are currently the most important. The Prospect Creek District southwest of Thompson Falls is of particular importance because of the presence of antimony-bearing quartz veins within Precambrian rocks. Here, mines are being developed by the U.S. Antimony Corporation.

If permission is granted by any claimholder to visit the mine dumps or tailings of any active or inactive mines in the region, specimens of stibnite, pyrrhotite, galena, and sphalerite can be found although most good specimens will probably be of thumbnail or micromount collection quality.

Access Information: Private land, patented and unpatented mining claims, National Forest Service land.

Useful Maps: U.S. Geogical Survey *Thompson Falls* Quadrangle, Montana; 15 Minute Series, Topographic, scale 1:62,500.

USDA Forest Service Forest Visitors Map; Lolo National Forest, Idaho and Montana.

Specific References:

Crowley, F. A. *Mines and Mineral Deposits (Except Fuels), Sanders County, Montana.* Montana Bureau of Mines and Geology Bulletin 34, pp. 26-35, 1963.

THOMPSON FALLS AREA

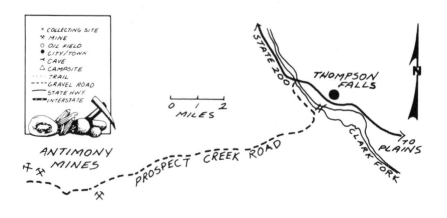

x COLLECTING SITE
* MINE
O OIL FIELD
• CITY/TOWN
< CAVE
△ CAMPSITE
···· TRAIL
---- GRAVEL ROAD
── STATE HWY
━━ INTERSTATE

0   1   2
MILES

STATE 200
THOMPSON FALLS
TO PLAINS
CLARK FORK
ANTIMONY MINES
PROSPECT CREEK ROAD

Glacier National Park

Very little that is new can be said of Glacier National Park, one of the most beautiful and spectacular regions in this country. Shaped by a combination of diastrophic and gradational forces, it presents broad U-shaped valleys, sharp conical peaks, and knife-like ridges that testify to past glacial epochs.

Close scrutiny of the ancient rocks reveal startling secrets of the park's geologic history. Layer upon layer of highly compressed sediments contain some very unusual and rarely preserved sedimentary features. Ripple marks, mud cracks, and rain drop impressions are relatively common. These features tell geologists that the vast thickness of sedimentary rock exposed here was deposited in a large basin which was slowly subsiding.

Perhaps the most interesting of the sedimentary features are the concentric ringed structures of fossil algae, possibly the oldest fossils in Montana. Particularly fine displays can be viewed in road cuts along Going To The Sun Highway about 8.8 miles west of Logan Pass. Collecting specimens of these features within the national park boundaries is strictly forbidden. Sediments of similar age do occur to the west and south of Glacier, and, on frequent occasions, reveal similar features, including fossil algae, and here specimens may be collected.

For the reader who is interested in learning more about the fascinating geology of Glacier National Park and the surrounding area, the following books are recommended: *The Geologic Story of Glacier National Park* and *Glaciers and Glaciation in Glacier National Park,* by James L. Dyson, and *Rocks, Ice and Water,* by David Alt and Donald Hyndman. Other references, mostly U.S. Geological Survey publications, are listed under "Specific References," but these provide a more technical description more appropriate to the reader with some geological background. Another book worth having is *Roadside Geology of Montana,* by David Alt and Donald Hyndman. It describes the geology that can be seen from the various highways as one travels through the park.

Travel through Glacier is seasonal. Although U.S. Highway 2 on the southern boundary of the park is open and maintained throughout the winter months, the more scenic Going To The Sun Highway (U.S. Highway 87) from St. Mary to West Glacier via Logan Pass is only open from late spring to late fall. Winter travel on the road is impossible because of deep snow and the threat of avalanches. Because of the spectacular scenery, a visit to Glacier should be reserved for the summer months.

Access Information: Federal land (National Park)—No Collecting!

Useful Maps: U.S. Geological Survey *Chief Mtn.* Quadrangle, Montana; 30 Minute Series, Topographic.

U.S. Geological Survey Glacier National Park Map; Scale 1:100,000.

USDA Forest Service Forest Visitors Map; Flathead National Forest (North Half), Montana.

Specific References:

Alt, David, and Hyndman, Donald. *Roadside Geology of Montana,* Missoula, Montana: Mountain Press Publishing Co., 1986, 427 pp.

Alt, David, and Hyndman, Donald. *Rocks, Ice and Water.* Missoula, Montana: Mountain Press Publishing Co., 1973.

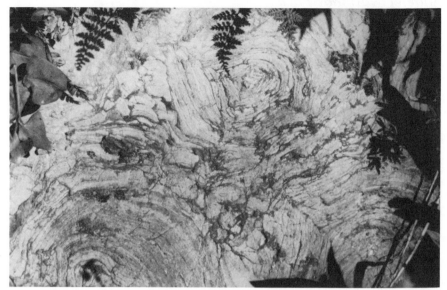
Fossil Algae near Logan Pass, Glacier National Park.

Dyson, J. L. *Glaciers and Glaciation in Glacier National Park.* Glacier Natural History Association Special Bulletin No. 2, 1966.

Dyson, J. L. *The Geologic Story of Glacier National Park.* Glacier Natural History Association Special Bulletin No. 3, 1969.

Rezak, Richard. *Stromatolites of the Belt Series in Glacier National Park and Vicinity, Montana.* U.S. Geological Survey Professional Paper 296, 1957.

Ross, C. P. and Rezak, Richard. *The Rocks and Fossils of Glacier National Park: The Story of Their Origin and History.* U.S. Geological Survey Professional Paper 294-K, 1959.

Ross, C. P. *Geology of Glacier National Park and the Flathead Region, Northwestern Montana.* U.S. Geological Survey Professional Paper 296, 1959.

Scardapane, F. A. "The Fossil Algae of Glacier National Park, Montana." *Rocks and Minerals,* Vol. 43, No. 10, October, 1968, pp. 729-734.

Kalispell Area

A considerable number of mines occur in areas to the north and south of Kalispell. Most are apparently small, and the deposits have produced relatively small quantities of copper, lead, and silver. The production records of these various mines cannot compare to those of the mining districts in the southwestern and western part of the state.

Since the mines are generally small, no specific locations are provided here. If the reader is interested in visiting the mines near Kalispell, Montana Bureau of Mines and Geology Bulletin 79 may provide the needed information.

An area west of Olney (twelve miles northwest of Whitefish on U.S. Highway 93) has produced some fine pseudomorphs of limonite after pyrite cubes. To reach the locality take Forest Road Number 60 south and west of Olney for 6.3 miles. Watch for a road on the right at this point. Take the road for a short distance to where it curves sharply. Near this curve, the blue-green rock contains some small but interesting pyrite cubes. Past this curve, where

LIMONITE WEST OF OLNEY

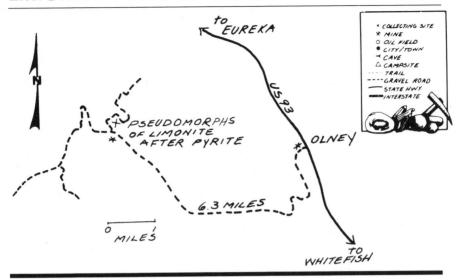

to EUREKA

US 93

PSEUDOMORPHS OF LIMONITE AFTER PYRITE

OLNEY

6.3 MILES

N

0 MILES 1

TO WHITEFISH

× COLLECTING SITE
✴ MINE
○ OIL FIELD
● CITY/TOWN
⌐ CAVE
△ CAMPSITE
····· TRAIL
---- GRAVEL ROAD
—— STATE HWY.
▬▬ INTERSTATE

HORN CORAL & CALCITE NORTH OF COLUMBIA FALLS

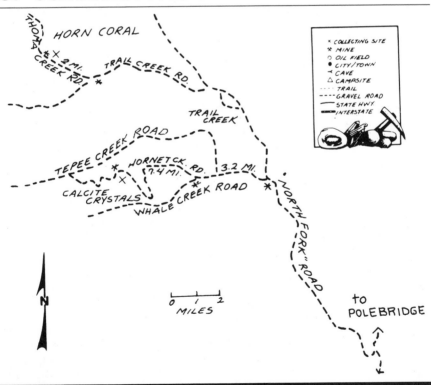

THOMA CREEK RD.

HORN CORAL

2 MI.

TRAIL CREEK RD.

TRAIL CREEK

TEPEE CREEK ROAD

HORNET CK. RD.

7.4 MI.

3.2 MI.

CALCITE CRYSTALS

WHALE CREEK ROAD

NORTH FORK" ROAD

N

0 1 2 MILES

to POLEBRIDGE

× COLLECTING SITE
✴ MINE
○ OIL FIELD
● CITY/TOWN
⌐ CAVE
△ CAMPSITE
····· TRAIL
---- GRAVEL ROAD
—— STATE HWY.
▬▬ INTERSTATE

the road begins to descend, limonite cubes may be dug from the weathered rock on the right. Watch for places where others have been digging.

Several other interesting localities are found a good distance north of Columbia Falls near the North Fork of the Flathead River. Specimens here include calcite crystals and horn corals. The directions to these localities are complex, but a good forest service map and the following description should help:

About ten miles north of Polebridge along the North Fork Road watch for the Whale Creek road junction. After turning left here, it is 3.2 miles along the Whale Creek road and an additional 7.4 miles along the Hornet Creek road to the locality where the calcite crystals may be found, exposed in high banks on the left side.

To reach the horn coral locality, continue north on the North Fork Road from Polebridge instead of turning left on the Whale Creek road. At Trail Creek turn left onto the Trail Creek road. The Thoma Creek road to the right is six miles west of the Trail Creek junction. Two miles up the Thoma Creek road there are several road cuts. The horn corals occur in the limestone exposed in the road cuts on the right.

Both of the localities listed above are reached by fairly good roads leading north from Columbia Falls, but local inquiry should be made if plans are made to visit these areas in the late spring or fall. They both exist at relatively high elevations and may be snowed in.

Access Information: National Forest Service land, patented and unpatented mining claims, private land.

Useful Maps: USDA Forest Service Forest Visitors Map; Flathead National Forest, (North Half), Montana.

Specific References:

Johns, W. M. *Geology and Mineral Deposits of Lincoln and Flathead Counties, Montana.* Montana Bureau of Mines and Geology Bulletin 79, pp. 126-146, 1970.

Taylor, A. V. and Shenon, P. J. *Geology and Ore Occurrences of the Hog Haven Mining District, Flathead County, Montana.* Montana Bureau of Mines and Geology Memoir 17 1936.

Libby Area

Mining began in this region with placer deposits worked for gold in the early 1880s. The oldest lode mine was developed about 1887, and since that time mining has been sporadic and apparently not extremely profitable. The mines are generally located about twenty miles south of Libby in the tributary valleys along the east slopes of the Cabinet Mountains and south of Troy (to the west of Libby). They are reached by a variety of good dirt and gravel roads leading up tributary valleys of the Kootenai River and Libby Creek.

Recently, a silver mine near Troy has been ranked as the largest in the United States. Several million ounces of silver have been mined during a short period of operation. Collectors might check locally concerning the mine, but it is doubtful that access to the dumps or tailings will be allowed.

The ores which contained the gold and other precious metals resulted from igneous intrusions into Precambrian Belt Series rocks predominant in the area. Gold, silver, lead, and some zinc were considered to be the most important metals, so dumps and tailings should produce galena, sphalerite, and pyrite.

LIBBY AREA

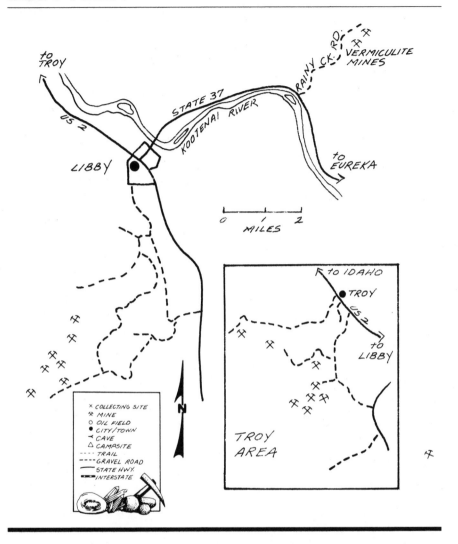

Extensive deposits of the hydrous biotite mica called vermiculite are presently being developed about seven miles northeast of Libby. Vermiculite, which expands when heated, has many uses, but it is primarily used as an insulation material. One of the more common and familiar product names for the expanded material is "Zonolite." This interesting and very useful mineral was first discovered about 1915. However, commercial production did not begin until 1925, when the Zonolite Company recovered it from open pits. The geology of the general area, the history of vermiculite production, and the history of the Zonolite Company itself are documented in Montana Bureau of Mines and Geology Memoir 27.

Since the vermiculite mine is in operation, access for collecting specimens is highly doubtful. A visit to the Zonolite Company's office may at least reward the interested rockhound with current information regarding the enterprise and the various processes necessary to produce the final product. Geologists employed by the company may be able to furnish information about potential sources of other rocks and minerals nearby.

Access Information: Private land, patented and unpatented mining claims, National Forest Service land.

Useful Maps: U.S. Geological Survey *Libby, Little Hoodoo Mtn., Troy* and *Vermiculite Mtn.* Quadrangles, Montana; 7.5 Minute Series, Topographic, scale 1:24,000.

USDA Forest Service Forest Visitors Map; Kootenai National Forest and East Half Kaniksu National Forest, Idaho and Montana.

Specific References:

Johns, W. M. *Geology and Mineral Deposits of Lincoln and Flathead Counties, Montana.* Montana Bureau of Mines and Geology Bulletin 79, pp. 85-105, 1970.

Pardee, J. T., and Larsen, E. S *Deposits of Vermiculite and Other Minerals in the Rainy Creek District near Libby, Montana.* U.S. Geological Survey Bulletin 805-B, 1929.

Perry, E. S. *Talc, Graphite, Vermiculite and Asbestos in Montana.* Montana Bureau of Mines and Geology Memoir 27, pp. 24-28, 1948.

MUSEUMS WITH DISPLAYS OF ROCKS, MINERALS, GEMSTONES, AND FOSSILS

"Rich with the spoils of Nature." Sir Thomas Browne (1605-1682)

Blaine County Museum

Although this museum in Chinook is devoted mainly to the human history of northern Montana, it houses one of the more outstanding paleontological displays in the state.

The most notable feature in the paleontology display is the restored skull of a *Gorgosaurus.* This large carnivorous dinosaur apparently roamed northern Montana and southern Canada during the Late Cretaceous Period.

Small, well constructed dioramas accompany many of the displays. The descriptions of specimens are very professional, making this a remarkable exhibit. Such a display is unusual for a relatively small county museum, and a visit here provides insight into the geologic history of north central Montana.

The museum is located four blocks south of U.S. Highway 2 in Chinook, and is open from May 1st through September 30th. Hours of operation are 9:00 a.m. to 5:00 p.m. Monday through Saturday, and noon to 4:00 p.m. Sunday. Times other than these are by appointment only. There is no admission charge, but donations will be accepted.

For additional information, write or call: Blaine County Museum, Box 927, Chinook, MT 59523, (406) 357-2590.

Carter County Museum

There is an extraordinary natural history display in the small town of Ekalaka. Once contained in the basement of the high school, the museum now occupies an attractive building on the north edge of town.

A six-foot-long *Triceratops* skull dominates the displays of many dinosaurs, all of which were found near Ekalaka. A specimen of distinctive importance is a plaster cast of the skull of *Pachycephalosaurus,* a rare "bone-headed" dinosaur also found near the town (the original specimen is in an eastern museum). Invertebrate fossils of many phyla are on display in showcases, but there are also collections of minerals (including an excellent display of fluorescent types), items of local historical interest, and several dioramas of local wildlife in a natural setting.

The museum is open all year from 8:00 a.m. to 5:00 p.m., Tuesday through Sunday. There is no admission charge, but donations are accepted to help defray expenses.

While in the Ekalaka area, rockhounds should visit Medicine Rocks State Park about ten miles north of town. It is a region in which sandstone cliffs and small buttes have been sculpted by wind and water. Many of the formations are spectacular and the strange shapes offer a great deal for the imagination. Camping is allowed in the park, but facilities are primitive.

For additional information, write: Carter County Museum, Ekalaka, MY 59324.

Earth Science Museum in Loma

The museum in Loma is dedicated to education in the earth sciences. Numerous, well-organized displays of minerals, lapidary work, paleontology, anthropology, and archaeology are offered for viewing.

There are several large mineral specimens, including locally collected concretions containing well-formed crystals of calcite. There are beautifully displayed cabinet specimens of numerous species of minerals, and dioramas illustrating the geologic and more recent history of the earth and relating it to the state of Montana. A display of Montana's official state gemstones includes sapphires from various localities (including the famed Yogo Gulch) and scenic dendritic Montana agate from the Yellowstone River. The displays are unusually excellent for a small private museum. A small gift shop is operated to help meet expenses.

The Earth Science Museum is located at 106 Main Street in Loma and is open daily from June to November. Hours of operation are 9:00 a.m. to 7:00 p.m. There is no admission charge, but donations are accepted.

For further information, write or call: Earth Science Museum, 106 Main Street, Loma, MT 59460, (406) 739-4357.

Fort Peck Museum

The power plant of a hydroelectric facility may seem like an odd place for a museum. Perhaps it is appropriate though, that this display resides where it does since most of it consists of fossils and artifacts collected in the immediate vicinity of Fort Peck at about the time the dam and powerhouse were being constructed. Represented are marine fossils from the Cretaceous Bearpaw Shale and various dinosaur remains from the Cretaceous Hell Creek Formation. A superb specimen of an Early Tertiary fresh water bony fish is one of the rarer specimens displayed.

Several vertebrate remains—a portion of a *Triceratops* skull, *Hadrosaur* skull, and the partial skeleton of a large *Mosasaur*—dominate the outstanding displays exhibited here. The history of Fort Peck itself is portrayed in various maps, photos, and artifacts. Tours of the hydroelectric plant can also be arranged.

The museum is located in Power Plant No. I and is open daily from Memorial Day to Labor Day. Hours of operation are from 8:30 a.m. to 5:30 p.m., with other times by appointment. There is no admission charge.

For further information, write: Fort Peck Museum, Corps of Engineers, Montana Area Office, Fort Peck, MT 59223.

"Mac's Museum" In Broadus

Mr. Mac McCurdy has spent a considerable number of years accumulating the various items which are presently housed in the Powder River County High School. A collection of minerals, fossils, and artifacts make up a large portion of the collection. The display of cabinet quality mineral specimens (as well as hand specimens for student study) rivals that of many small university geology departments. Fossils in the display include locally collected ammonites, bison, and mammoth remains.

An entire wall is devoted to artifacts. Most of this display consists of picture frames containing numerous arrowheads and similar tools from localities in Montana and other states.

Perhaps the most outstanding aspect of the museum is one of the more complete collections of modern shells in the nation. Display cases and many cabinet drawers are filled with the shells of various families of gastropods and pelecypods, along with some echinoderms and crustaceans, with unforgettable patterns and colors.

Since the museum is located within a school building, the season and hours of operation are the same as those for the school. Other times are by appointment. No admission is charged. For more information, write or call: Powder River County High School, Broadus, MT 59317, (406) 436-2658.

Montana Tech Mineral Museum and World Museum of Mining

One of the more outstanding mineral displays in the nation is located on the campus of the Montana College of Mineral Science and Technology in Butte. Displayed are striking specimens of minerals from the Butte mines, minerals from other mining areas in Montana, and minerals from famous ore deposits located throughout the world.

Only about ten percent of the entire school collection is on display, but it must represent the more spectacular specimens. In a separate room, fluorescent minerals from many localities (fluorescent under either long or short-wave ultraviolet light) can be viewed.

The museum is most easily reached by driving west on Park Street to the Montana Tech Campus. Signs will direct you to the museum and the many available parking lots.

The hours of operation are 8:00 a.m. to 5:00 p.m., seven days a week, from June 1st through Labor Day. During the remainder of the year, the museum is open only on weekdays. There is no admission charge. The museum is highly recommended for the rockhound who is particularly enthusiastic about minerals.

Located about .5 mile west of the Montana Tech Campus near the end of Park Street is the World Museum of Mining and Hellroaring Gulch, a unique display of mining methods and equipment. It is open from 9:00 a.m. to 9:00 p.m. daily from June 1st to Labor Day. With the exception of December, January, and February, it is open the rest of the year from 10:00 a.m. to 5:00 p.m., Tuesday through Sunday. There is no admission charge.

For more information, write or call: Mineral Museum, Montana College of Mineral Science and Technology, Butte, MT 59701, (406) 792-8321.

Museum of the Rockies

The Museum of the Rockies has implemented a program whereby many of the exotic paleontological finds, which at one time could only be collected by and displayed in large eastern museums, can now be retained in Montana. The staff at the museum is trained in vertebrate paleontology, and has made some phenomenal acquisitions.

A large *Triceratops* skull collected near the Fort Peck Reservoir a few years ago initiated the natural history section. Since then, there have been important new finds. Skeletal remains of *Tyrannosaurus rex* have recently been discovered in the Jordan area, and if the specimen proves to be relatively complete, the museum will be one of the very few in the world to have a reconstructed skeleton on display.

The incredible discovery of baby dinosaurs and fossil eggs near Choteau has also contributed to the reputation of this museum. Restorations of the dinosaurs recovered there and a nest of eggs are on display.

The museum has the potential of becoming one of the better paleontological displays in the northwest, especially given the enthusiasm of the staff, but it is noted for more than just the paleontological exhibits. There are numerous displays of western art, local history, Plains Indian culture, and unique archaeological finds, as well as a gift shop.

The Museum of the Rockies is located on the Montana State University Campus, near the football stadium on the corner of S. 7th Ave., and Kagy Blvd. Hours are 9:00 a.m. to 4:30 p.m., Monday through Friday, and 1:00 p.m. to 4:30 p.m., Saturday and Sunday, except on national holidays. During the winter the museum is closed on Mondays.

For additional information, write or call: Museum of the Rockies, Montana State University, Bozeman, MT 59717, (406) 994-2251.

APPENDIX A

General References

Some of the following books and magazines were referred to briefly in the introduction and chapters dealing with Montana's geologic story and official state gemstones. They are listed here, along with others, for the benefit of those who wish to do additional reading.

Books

Alt, David., and Hyndman, Donald W. *Roadside Geology of Montana*. Missoula, Montana: Mountain Press Publishing Co., 1986, 427 pp.

Ballantyne, Verne. *How and Where to Find Gold*. New York: Arco Publishing Co. 1980, 122 pp.

Campbell, N. P. *Caves of Montana*. Montana Bureau of Mines and Geology Bulletin 105, 1978.

Dingman, O. A. *Placer Mining Possibilities in Montana*. Montana Bureau of Mines and Geology Memoir 5, 1932.

Earll, F. N., et. al. *Handbook for Small Mining Enterprises*. Montana Bureau of Mines and Geology Bulletin 99, 1976.

Fenton, C. L., and Fenton, M. A. *The Fossil Book*. Garden City, New York: Doubleday and Company, Inc., 1958, 482 pp.

Glasscock, C. B. *The War of the Copper Kings*. New York: Grosset Publishing Company, 1935, 314 pp.

Hanson, J. E. *Gold Secrets of Mystical Montana: A Manual for the Recreational Prospector*. South Carolina: Priority Research, 1982.

Jackson, H. M., et. al. *Mineral and Water Resources of Montana*. Montana Bureau of Mines and Geology Special Publication 28, 1963.

Lanham, Url. *The Bone Hunters* New York: Columbia University Press, 1973, 285 pp.

Lawson, D. C. *Directory of Montana Mining Enterprises for 1980.* Montana Bureau of Mines and Geology Bulletin 115, 1981.

Lyden, C. J. *The Gold Placers of Montana.* Montana Bureau of Mines and Geology Memoir 26, 1948.

MacFall, Russell, and Wollin, Jay. *Fossils for Amateurs.* New York: Van Nostrand-Reinhold Company, 1972, 341 pp.

Perry, E. S. *Montana in the Geologic Past.* Montana Bureau of Mines and Geology Bulletin 26, 1962.

Renfro, H. B., and Feray, D. E. *Geological Highway Map of the Northern Rocky Mountain Region* (Map No. 5). Tulsa, Oklahoma: American Association of Petroleum Geologists, 1962.

Sales, R. H. *Underground Warfare at Butte.* Caldwell, Idaho: The Caxton Printers, 1966, 77 pp.

Sanbourn, William. *The Handbook of Crystal and Mineral Collecting.* Mentone, California: Gembooks, 1966, 81 pp.

Sinkankas, John. *Prospecting for Gemstones and Minerals.* New York: Van Nostrand-Reinhold Company, 1970, 397 pp.

Stone, Gergory V. *Prospecting for Lode Gold.* Philadelphia, Pennsylvania: Dorrance and Company, 1975, 50 pp.

Stout, K. S. *Montana Mining Law.* Bureau of Mines and Geology Bulletin 22, 1961.

Wolle, M. S. *Montana Pay Dirt: A Guide to the Mining Camps of the Treasure State.* Denver, Colorado: Sage Books, 1963, 436 pp.

Magazine Articles

Eichhorn, L. C. "Montana Baculites," *Gems and Minerals,* No. 425, February, 1973, pp. 34-35.

Field, L. G. "Southeastern Montana; The Neglected Area," *Lapidary Journal,* Vol. 36, No. 12, March, 1983, pp. 1992-1997.

Jones, W. R. "How to Use Topo Maps," *Gems and Minerals,* No. 448 and No. 449, February and March, 1975.

Kraus, P. D. "Sapphire—Birthstone for September," *Lapidary Journal,* Vol. 31, No. 6, September, 1977, pp. 1404-1412.

Rosenhouse, Leo. "Quest for Montana Sapphire," *Gems and Minerals,* No. 478, August, 1977, pp. 44-71.

Shaub, B. M. "Genesis of Agates, Geodes, Septaria and other Concretions of Sedimentary Origin (Part One)," *Lapidary Journal,* Vol. 34, No. 3, June, 1980, pp. 650-679.

Shaub, B. M. "Genesis of Agates, Geodes, Septaria and other Concretions of Sedimentary Origin (Part Two)," *Lapidary Journal,* Vol. 34, No. 4, July, 1980, pp. 860-896.

Wilson, M. M. "Montana's Treasure", *Lapidary Journal,* Vol. 30, No. I and No. 2, April and May, 1976.

Wilson, M. W. "Sapphire Blue," *Lapidary Journal,* Vol. 31, No. 1, April, 1977, pp. 3244.

Wurfel, D. M. "Mining the Montana Sapphire—A Collector's Guide to Five Mines," *Lapidary Journal,* Vol. 33, No. 4, July, 1979, pp. 952-955.

Zeitner, J. C. "The Big Sky Sapphire," *Lapidary Journal,* Vol. 32, No. 6, September, 1978, pp. 1244-1254.

APPENDIX B

Rock Shops In Montana

A current list of rock shops is difficult to keep because old shops often go out of business for one reason or another, and new shops open. This list represents shops which were open at the time the research for this book was being conducted. Telephone numbers have been provided for most, and it is suggested that you phone before traveling out of your way to visit it.

The proprietors of these shops are excellent resource persons and can often provide information about local gem, mineral, or fossil collecting sites.

Billings
Grand Frame
1010 Grand Avenue
Billings, MT 59102
(406) 248-3718

Hobby Cab Rock Shop
1912 Old Hardin Road
Billings, MT 59101
(406) 256-5044

Greenleafs
312 8th Street West
Billings, MT 59102
(406) 245-7424

Collector's Emporium
114 North 29th
Billings, MT 59101
(406) 259-2338

Bozeman
Earth Treasures
523 B Professional Dr.
Bozeman, MT 59715
(406) 586-3451

Butte
DJ Minerals
1001 S. Montana
Butte, MT 59715
(406) 782-7339

Trevillion-Johnson Gems
2400 S. Montana
Butte, MT 59701
(406) 723-6010

Butte Copper Co.
3015 Harrison Ave.
Butte, MT 59701
(406) 494-2070

East Helena
Johnson Jewlers
3251 Canyon Ferry Rd.
East Helena, MT 59636
(406) 227-5529

Helena
The Prospector Shop
6312 W. US Hwy 12
Helena, MT 59601
(406) 442-1872

Ennis
Ennis Rock House
P.O. Box 293
Ennis, MT 59729
(406) 682-4689

Gallatin Gateway
Assay Office
P.O. Box 379
Gallatin Gateway, MT 59730
(406) 585-1300

Great Falls
Agate Shop
925 NW BYP
Great Falls, MT 59404
(406) 771-1032

Laurel
Van Bieber Rock and Antiques
207 West Main
Laurel, MT 59044
(406) 628-4982

Livingston
Gil's Indian Trading Post
207 West Park
Livingston, MT 59047
(406) 222-0112

Park Rock Shop
2 miles south on Hwy 89
P.O. Box 368
Livingston, MT 59047

Missoula
Jem Shoppe and Custom Jewelry
105 S. Higgins Ave.
Missoula, MT 59802
(406) 728-4077

Chalet Jewelers
2946 N. Reserve
Missoula, MT 59802
(406) 549-5771

Sidney
Frandsen's Agates
1115 North Central Ave
P.O. Box 706
Sidney, MT 59270
(406) 482-2183

Virginia City
115 W. Wallace
Virginia City, MT 59755
(406) 843-5345

West Yellowstone
Visitor's Bureau Gift Shop
107 Canyon Street
West Yellowstone, MT 59758
(406) 646-7831

APPENDIX C

Rock Clubs In Montana

The following list of rock clubs provides a minimum amount of information and is limited to current mailing addresses. Information concerning meeting places and times can be obtained by writing directly to the clubs or referring to a current edition of the "Membership Directory of Northwest Federation of Mineralogical Societies."

Most club members are always anxious to greet visitors, and are often willing to share and exchange information concerning potential sources of gem, mineral, and fossil specimens.

Big Sky Facetors Guild, Inc.
P.O. Box 564
Great Falls, MT 59403

Big Sky Rock and Mineral Club
P.O. Box 1126
Polson, MT 59860

Billings Gem and Mineral Club
P.O. Box 477
Billings, MT 59101

Bozeman Gem and Mineral Club
P.O. Box 375
Bozeman, MT 59715

Butte Mineral and Gem Club
P.O. Box 4492
Butte, MT 59701

Central Gem and Mineral Society
P.O. Box 871
Lewistown, MT 59456

Charles M. Russell Gem
   and Mineral Society
P.O. Box 61
St. Marie, MT 59321

Hellgate Mineral Society
P.O. Box 2683
Missoula, MT 59806-2683

Kalispell Rockhounds
379 Managham Ln
Kalispell, MT 59901

Lewistown Rockers
P.O. Box 871
Lewistown, MT 59457

Musselshell Mineral and
   Fossil Society
168-43 U.S. Hwy 12
Roundup, MT 59072-1837

Yellowstone Agate Club
1001 N. Haynes
Miles City, MT 59301

Yellowstone Gem and
   Mineral Society
Rte. 38 Box 2039
Livingston, MT 59047

APPENDIX D

Finding Maps and Information

The following agencies and institutions can often answer questions by mail. Many publish maps which can be extremely useful in determining land ownership. To obtain maps, first request an index of map titles.

The Montana Bureau of Mines and Geology and the U.S. Geological Survey have printed numerous technical publications concerning the geology of Montana, and many are available at libraries in some of Montana's larger cities. The libraries of colleges and universities are also a source of these publications.

Bureau of Land Management
Montana State Office
Granite Tower Building
222 N. 32nd Street
Billings, MT 59107

Department of Earth Sciences
Montana State University
Bozeman, MT 59717

Department of Geology
University of Montana
Missoula, MT 59801

Montana Bureau of Mines and
   Geology
Montana Tech
Main Hall, Room 206
Butte, MT 59701

U.S. Department of Agriculture
Forest Service
Regional Office
Missoula, MT 59801

U.S. Geological Survey Books:
   Eastern Distribution Branch
Text Products Section
U.S. Geological Survey
604 South Picket Street
Alexandria, VA 22304

U.S. Geological Survey Maps:
Western Distribution Branch
U.S. Geological Survey
Box 25286, Federal Center
Denver, CO 80225

GLOSSARY OF TERMS

AMMONITE - An extinct group of mollusks which may have been similar to the present-day chambered nautilus.

AMPHIBOLE - A complex silicate mineral group.

ANHEDRAL - A crystal with no well-developed geometric faces.

ANTICLINE - An up-turned fold in the rocks of the earth's crust.

BATHOLITH - A large mass of plutonic rock many tens of square miles in area.

BEDDING PLANE - The plane which separates individual layers of rock.

BELEMNITE - An extinct cephalopod possessing a cigar-shaped protective guard.

BRACHIOPOD - A marine animal with two unequal shells showing bilateral symmetry.

BRECCIA - Angular rock fragments cemented into solid rock.

BRYOZOANS - Small colonial animals which build calcareous structures in which they live.

CABOCHON - A gemstone which has been fashioned into a dome and polished.

CEPHALOPODS - A class of mollusks which includes the squid, the octopus, and the chambered nautilus.

CHALCEDONY - A microcrystalline variety of quartz.

CHERT - An extremely fine-grained siliceous rock exhibiting many colors.

COLUMNAL - A portion of the column or "stem" of a crinoid.

CONCRETION - A nodular lumpy rock, generally sedimentary, which forms about a nucleus (often a fossil).

CRINOID - A "flower-like" echinoderm with a multi-armed calyx or head and a long column or "stem" attaching it to the sea floor.

DENDRITE - A tree-like pattern produced when minerals (usually oxides of manganese) crystallize in minute fractures in rocks.

DIASTROPHIC - Natural processes which deform the earth's crust (tension and compression) producing faults, folds, etc.

DIKE - An igneous intrusion which cuts across pre-existing rock layers.

ECHINODERM - A phylum of marine invertebrates with spiny bodies, including starfishes, sea urchins, and sea cucumbers.

ECHINOIDS - A class of echinoderms which includes the sand dollar and sea urchin.

EUHEDRAL - A crystal with well developed geometric faces.

FAULT - A break or fracture in the earth's crust along which movement takes place.

FLOWSTONE - Calcite deposits formed along the walls of caverns where water carrying dissolved minerals "flow" from the rock.

FOSSIL - The remains of plants or animals preserved in rock.

FUMEROLE - Hydrothermal activity where large quantities of steam are released into the air from a high pressure ground water source.

GASTROPOD - A type of mollusk with an asymmetrical unchambered shell.

GENERA - (Plural for genus).

GENUS - One of the divisions in the classification of living things (or fossils).

GEOLOGY - The science which studies the earth, its composition, the processes which affects the rocks of which it is composed, and its history.

GEOMORPHOLOGY - The geologic study which deals with the shape of the earth's surface and the development of landforms.

GRADATION - A natural process such as weathering, erosion, or deposition which helps to shape the surface of the earth.

HYDROTHERMAL - Processes involving the action of hot water solutions.

IGNEOUS - Rock which has hardened from a molten state.

INTRUSION - Igneous rock which was intruded into pre-exisitng rocks.

LACCOLITH - A igneous intrusion which has squeezed between older rock layers and domed up the overlying strata.

LAPIDARY - An artist who fashions gemstones from rough rock.

LODE - A mineral deposit contained in bedrock.

METAMORPHIC - Rocks which have undergone physical and chemical change due to extreme changes in temperature and pressure.

MIAROLITIC - Small cavities in igneous (granitic) rocks often containing crystals of different rock-making minerals.

MICROMOUNT - Mineral specimens which have been permanently mounted and best observed with the aid of a microscope.

MOLLUSK - The group of invertebrate animals to which belong the cephalopods, pelecypods, gastropods, etc.

MOSASAUR - An extinct swimming reptile which inhabited the Late Cretaceous seas.

PALEONTOLOGY - The branch of science which deals with the study of fossils.

PELECYPODS - A class of bivalve molusks which includes the oyster and clams.

PHENOCRYSTS - The larger crystals in a porphyritic rock.

PHYSIOGRAPHY - The shape of the land; study of landforms.

PLACER - Generally a sand or gravel deposit containing minerals of economic value.

PLUTONIC - Igneous rocks which hardened deep within the crust of the earth.

PORPHYRY - An igneous rock with crystals of different size—usually large crystals surrounded by very small crystals.

PSEUDOMORPH - A crystal with the geometric form of a mineral which has been replaced chemically by another mineral.

SEDIMENTARY - Rocks which form from the accumulation, compaction and cementation of sediment.

SEDIMENTOLOGY - The scientific study of sedimentary rocks, their composition, and their origin.

SEPTARIAN CONCRETION - A concretion possessing internal fractures which are filled or partially filled with minerals.

SILICEOUS - Containing silica.

SILL - An igneous intrusion which parallels pre-existing rock layers.

SPELEOTHEMS - Mineral deposits of a secondary nature found in caves.

SPIRIFER - A type of brachiopod possessing a butterfly-shaped shell.

STALACTITE - An icicle-like deposit which hangs from the ceiling of a cavern.

STALAGMITE - An icicle-like deposit which builds up from the floor of a cavern.

STRATIGRAPHY - The scientific study of the layers of strata in the earth's crust.

STREAM PIRACY - The diverting of water from a stream due to its capture by the headward erosion of a nearby stream.

SYNCLINE - A down-turned fold in the rocks of the earth's crust.

THUMBNAIL SPECIMEN - A small mineral specimen about one inch by one inch in size.

TRILOBITE - Extinct marine arthropod which is beetle-like in appearance.

VOLCANIC - Igneous rocks which hardened on the earth's surface.

VUG - A small cavity in a rock.